BUSINESS, TECHNOLOGY AND FINANCE

SHADOW BANKING AND U.S. FINANCIAL REGULATORY POLICY

OVERVIEWS

BUSINESS, TECHNOLOGY AND FINANCE

Additional books in this series can be found on Nova's website under the Series tab.

Additional E-books in this series can be found on Nova's website under the E-book tab.

BUSINESS, TECHNOLOGY AND FINANCE

SHADOW BANKING AND U.S. FINANCIAL REGULATORY POLICY

OVERVIEWS

VIVIAN KELEMEN
EDITOR

NOVINKA
New York

For permission to use material from this book please contact us:
Telephone 631-231-7269; Fax 631-231-8175
Web Site: http://www.novapublishers.com

Library of Congress Cataloging-in-Publication Data

ISBN: 978-1-63117-527-5

Published by Nova Science Publishers, Inc. † New York

CONTENTS

Preface		**vii**
Chapter 1	Shadow Banking: Background and Policy Issues *Edward V. Murphy*	**1**
Chapter 2	Who Regulates Whom and How? An Overview of U.S. Financial Regulatory Policy for Banking and Securities Markets *Edward V. Murphy*	**35**
Index		**103**

PREFACE

This book develops a general framework for analyzing financial intermediation, and applies these concepts to several specific shadow banking sectors. The book focuses on comparing and contrasting the fundamental economic problems of simple banking and associated policy responses to analogous problems and policy proposals in shadow banking.

Chapter 1 – Shadow banking refers to financial firms and activities that perform similar functions to those of depository banks. Although the term is used to describe dissimilar firms and activities, a general policy concern is that a component of shadow banking could be a source of financial instability, even though that component might not be subject to regulations designed to prevent a crisis, or be eligible for emergency facilities designed to mitigate financial turmoil once it has begun. This concern is magnified by the experience of 2007-2009, during which financial problems among nonbank lenders, and disruption to securitization (in which both banks and nonbanks participated), contributed to the magnitude of the financial crisis. This report provides a framework for understanding shadow banking, discusses several fundamental problems of financial intermediation, and describes the experiences of several specific sectors of shadow banking during the financial crisis and related policy concerns.

Chapter 2 – Financial regulatory policies are of interest to Congress because firms, consumers, and governments fund many of their activities through banks and securities markets. Furthermore, financial instability can damage the broader economy. Financial regulation is intended to protect borrowers and investors that participate in financial markets and mitigate financial instability. This report provides an overview of the regulatory policies of the agencies that oversee banking and securities markets and explains which agencies are responsible for which institutions, activities, and markets. Some agencies regulate particular types of institutions for risky behavior or conflicts of interest, some agencies promulgate rules for certain financial transactions no matter what kind of institution engages in them, and other agencies enforce existing rules for some institutions, but not for others. These regulatory activities are not necessarily mutually exclusive.

In: Shadow Banking ...
Editor: Vivian Kelemen

ISBN: 978-1-63117-527-5

Chapter 1

SHADOW BANKING: BACKGROUND AND POLICY ISSUES*

Edward V. Murphy

SUMMARY

Shadow banking refers to financial firms and activities that perform similar functions to those of depository banks. Although the term is used to describe dissimilar firms and activities, a general policy concern is that a component of shadow banking could be a source of financial instability, even though that component might not be subject to regulations designed to prevent a crisis, or be eligible for emergency facilities designed to mitigate financial turmoil once it has begun. This concern is magnified by the experience of 2007-2009, during which financial problems among nonbank lenders, and disruption to securitization (in which both banks and nonbanks participated), contributed to the magnitude of the financial crisis. This report provides a framework for understanding shadow banking, discusses several fundamental problems of financial intermediation, and describes the experiences of several specific sectors of shadow banking during the financial crisis and related policy concerns.

---

* This is an edited, reformatted and augmented version of a Congressional Research Service publication, CRS Report for Congress R43345, dated December 31, 2013.

Shadow banking is contrasted with *luminated banking*, a term which the report uses to describe chartered banks that gather funds from depositors in order to offer loans that the chartered bank holds itself. Luminated banking, like all forms of financial intermediation, is subject to well- known risks, including credit risk, interest rate risk, maturity mismatch, and the potential for runs. Each sector of shadow banking is generally subject to the same problem of financial intermediation to which the sector is analogous. For example, if a sector of shadow banking such as money market funds (MMF) has investors that are analogous to depositors in luminated banking, then the potential for runs may be similar. Or, if the sector relies on collateralized loans, such as asset-backed commercial paper (ABCP), then disruptions in the market for the underlying collateral can cause fire sales that may reinforce and magnify price declines.

The regulatory regime and eligibility for emergency financial assistance for shadow banking varies from sector to sector and type of firm to type of firm. For example, the Dodd-Frank Act subjects certain large nonbank firms funded by repurchase agreements (repos) to safety and soundness regulation similar to banks. The Dodd-Frank Act prohibits emergency assistance to individual firms as was done in 2008 for Bear Stearns or AIG, but preserves the ability of the Federal Reserve to provide more generally eligible assistance to shadow banking sectors such as ABCP through the Term Asset Backed Liquidity Facility (TALF). Title II of the Dodd-Frank Act allows the FDIC to resolve the failure of any firm, including shadow banking firms, whose failure may pose a threat to financial stability.

Several components of shadow banking rely on securities markets to fund debt. These securities regulations are typically activity based, applying to all securities market participants if there is no explicit exemption. Securities regulation requires disclosure of material risks, but often does not attempt to limit the risks of firms funded through securities markets. In contrast, banking regulation sometimes applies only to firms with specific charters. Furthermore, banking regulators oversee linkages between banks, such as the payment system. Thus, debt funded through securities markets is likely to be subject to regulation no matter who does it, but that regulation is unlikely to be risk-based or to incorporate linkages between firms. Banking regulation is likely to be risk based, but to miss debt funded through securities markets.

Some policy options for shadow banking firms and markets are often analogous to policy options for depository banking or securities markets. Firms that engage in shadow banking could be subjected to safety and soundness regulation and capital requirements in order to limit risk and encourage resilience. Providers of short-term credit to shadow banks could be offered guarantees analogous to deposit insurance in order to minimize runs. Non-bank firms that rely on short-term credit to fund lending (or the holding of debt) can be made eligible for emergency lending facilities from a lender of last resort in order to address liquidity problems.

There are alternatives to the banking approach. Banks and other firms that fund themselves with substitute for deposits could be assessed higher fees to account for potential systemic costs that current market prices might not incorporate. More financial regulation could be made activity based, rather than charter based, in order to lessen regulatory arbitrage. Differences in banking regulation and securities regulation for the funding of debt could be preserved, but each separate category of regulation could be addressed where it applies.

The report analyzes five sectors of shadow banking. These sectors include (1) repos, (2) non-bank intermediaries, (3) ABCP, (4) securitization, and (5) MMFs. For each of these sectors, the report briefly defines the sector, recounts the sector's experience during the financial crisis, and outlines some related policy concerns. Each policy problem is described in the context of the general problems of financial intermediation introduced earlier in the report.

One view of the financial crisis of 2007-2008 is that it was not centered in traditional banking.[1] The term *shadow banking* " ... refers to credit intermediation involving leverage and maturity transformation that is partly or wholly outside the traditional banking system."[2] That is, shadow banking substitutes at least partially for simple banking in the creation and funding of debt. Several components of the shadow banking system contributed to the breadth of the financial turmoil that began in 2007, and the magnitude of the financial panic in September 2008, according to the Financial Crisis Inquiry Commission (FCIC).[3] In response, regulatory policymakers have been analyzing how the shadow banking system works, and considering options to promote greater financial stability in shadow banking.[4] Congress is considering several shadow banking regulatory reform proposals (e.g. changing the status of repurchase agreements [repos] in bankruptcy proceedings), overseeing related agency rulemaking (e.g., regulations for Money Market Funds [MMFs]), and overseeing the implementation of related financial reform legislation (e.g. applying the capital requirements in Section 171 of the Dodd-Frank Act to nonbanks).

This report develops a general framework for analyzing financial intermediation, and applies these concepts to several specific shadow banking sectors. The report focuses on comparing and contrasting the fundamental economic problems of simple banking (which will be referred to as *luminated banking*) and associated policy responses to analogous problems and policy proposals in shadow banking. Shadow banking provides a similar general service (financial intermediation) as luminated banking, and is subject to similar fundamental economic problems. Furthermore, many of the proposed regulatory responses for shadow banking have policy trade-offs analogous to regulatory policies in banking, and some shadow banking sectors already have a financial regulatory regime (such as securities regulations). Many of these economic problems and potential policy responses are illustrated by the experiences of five shadow banking sectors (repos, nonbanks, asset backed commercial paper [ABCP], securitization, and MMFs) during 2007-2008, and by regulatory responses currently being considered.[5]

Similarities and differences between securities market regulation and banking regulation can influence the size and stability of the financial system. In many cases (but not all), the kind of regulation applied to securities market activities is fundamentally different from the regulation of chartered depository banks. Banking regulation is typically applied only to specific institutions, is risk-based, takes into account the linkages between banks through the payment system, and includes government emergency backstops, such as a lender of last resort and a deposit guarantor. Securities regulation, which several categories of shadow banking involves, generally requires disclosure of material risks, but typically does not limit the risk that sophisticated securities market participants may take. On the other hand, the regulation of securities is often product and activity based, and therefore may adapt to financial innovations in which debt-related securities are offered by new kinds of business entities. Differences in these regulatory regimes can affect the degree to which debt is created through banking or shadow banking. The diversity of shadow banking activities and institutions makes it difficult to generalize; however, the degree to which debt financing in the financial system is covered by risk-based regulation, has access to emergency backstops, or can easily adapt to innovation in the provision of similar services may be influenced by regulatory choices for banking and shadow banking. By extension, changes to the regulation of shadow banking can affect the relative stability of the overall financial system.

The organization of the report is as follows. The report defines luminated banking and shadow banking, and identifies several common sources of financial instability from an economic perspective.[6] The report describes some of the standard economic tools (including regulations and emergency support) that are often applied to banking. It then describes five major components of shadow banking, and for each one, recounts its experience during the financial turmoil of 2007-2008 and analyzes policy proposals to change the regulatory approach and emergency support for that sector. The policy proposals are related back to analogous policy proposals in banking regulation.

DEFINING LUMINATED BANKING AND SHADOW BANKING

Defining "shadow banking" is difficult because defining banking is difficult.[7] Some analysts might be tempted to define banking as whatever firms with bank charters do; however, policy discussions of shadow banking include activities in which chartered banks participate, sometimes only with each other.[8] Therefore, a definition that is based on functions may be more useful for policy analysis, but even the functional definitions offered by various researchers have varied significantly, with important implications for what gets included under the label "shadow banking."[9] This report will follow a functional definition, seeking to provide a framework for analyzing several large sectors of the financial system that are usually included under the rubric "shadow banking," yet excludes insured deposits of chartered banks that hold their loans.

In broad terms, both banking and shadow banking provide the same service, which is financial intermediation. Financial intermediation includes gathering funds from savers, screening and qualifying applicants for funds, issuing and holding financial assets, and coordinating the payment of returns to savers. Shadow banking involves providing this financial intermediation with at least one difference from simple banking. In many cases (but not all), that difference involves reliance on securities markets to fund loans.

If shadow banking has at least one difference from simple banking, what is simple banking? Simple banking, or luminated banking, has each of the following four elements. The first row of **Figure 1** illustrates the flow of funds connecting savers and borrowers in a luminated banking business model. Luminated banks

1. gather funds in the form of deposits (time and transaction)
2. have special business charters identifying them as depositories
3. offer loans (and screen applicants)
4. hold the loans they originate. Repayments of loans fund the interest for depositors.

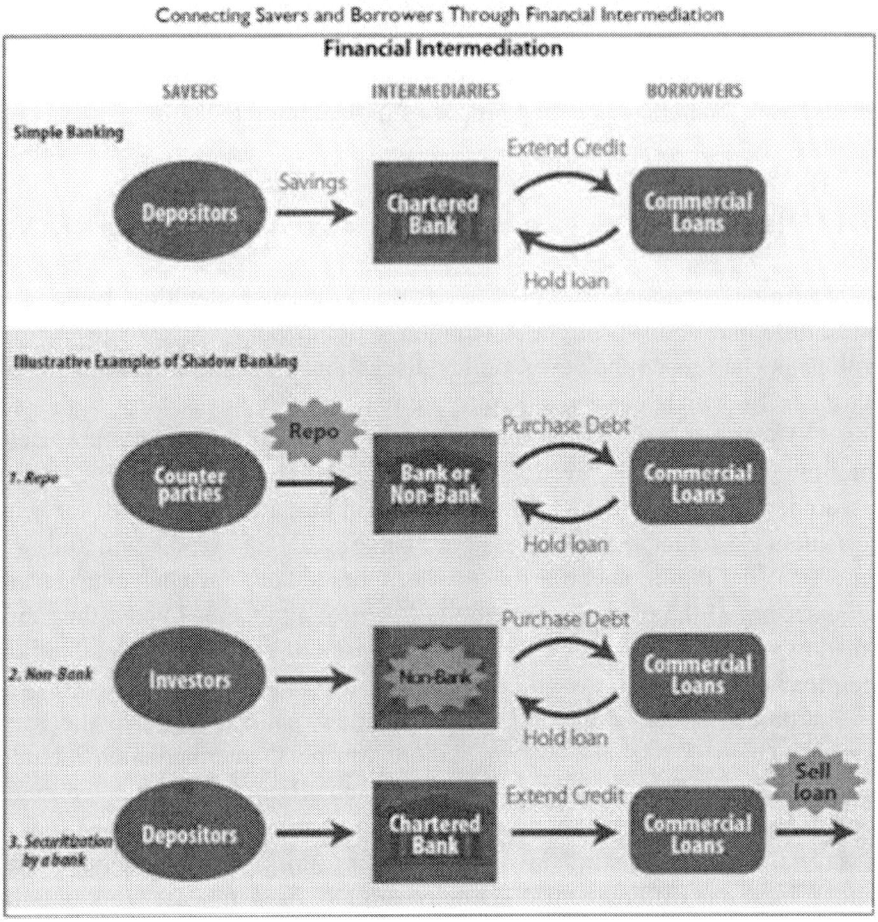

Source: CRS.

Notes: This is not an exhaustive list of monetary flows in financial intermediation. The flows show parallels between shadow banking and simple banking, and the stars show which part of financial intermediation a given shadow banking feature substitutes for a simple banking practice.

Figure 1. Examples of Banking and Shadow Banking.

The term shadow banking has been used to describe a variety of firms and activities that have little in common. However, they each differ in an at least one respect from the simple conception of banking illustrated in the first row of **Figure 1**. In this illustration, the term luminated banking is being used to describe a simple form of the "originate-to-hold" model of depository banking. In **Figure 1**, each following row provides an illustrative example of an activity or firm that deviates from luminated banking in at least one respect, yet provides similar financial intermediation. Adjusting the focal point of intermediation from left to right, the first shadow banking example in **Figure 1** illustrates a substitute for deposits (in this case repos), the second shadow banking example illustrates a substitute for firms with special bank charters (non-bank intermediaries), and the third row illustrates a substitute for holding loans (in this case selling loans through securitization).

The following five examples are a non-exhaustive list of shadow banking sectors. This list is included because each of these sectors will be addressed more fully in the policy analysis section of the report. They are presented here to see how each fits into the general concept of financial intermediation and how each differs from, or can be incorporated in, simple banking.

- (A) The Repo Market—Rather than gathering funds from depositors, some chartered banks (and nonbanks) borrow through repurchase agreements (repos, discussed more fully below). In a repo, a firm sells a security today with a promise to repurchase the security at a later date for a specified price. The time span and price differences are analogous to a loan and interest. Repos differ from simple banking in the way in which intermediaries gather funds from savers. Financial firms that fund themselves with repos may or may not have bank charters, may or may not extend credit or purchase debt, and may or may not hold the loans they originate. However, the first row of **Figure 1** shows that if a chartered bank borrows through repo markets (rather than deposits) in order to fund its lending activity, the financial intermediation is very similar to luminated banking. Furthermore, firms without bank charters can also gather funds from savers through repos.
- (B) Firms without bank charters—A firm does not have to be a chartered bank in order to borrow or lend, and luminated banking involves borrowing from depositors in order to offer and hold loans. In a trivial, but highly illustrative example, there was an ice cream shop in Pennsylvania that accepted deposits and offered loans.[10] Trusts and non-depository investment banks are more common than ice cream shops that offer banking services. The second row of **Figure 1** shows that if a firm without a bank charter funds itself with deposit-like loans while at the same time extending credit or purchasing debt, the resulting financial intermediation is very similar to luminated banking.

- (C) Commercial Paper—Firms do not have to go to banks to in order to borrow. Debt can be issued and traded through securities markets. Rather than originate and hold individual loans, chartered banks (and nonbanks) have at times sponsored interests in commercial paper, which is an example of marketable debt. One common form is to issue asset-backed commercial paper (ABCP), in which the commercial loans serve as collateral for shorter term debt issued in securities markets. Although not depicted in **Figure 1**, ABCP represents relatively short term borrowing (on the deposit side of financial intermediation) that is used to acquire and fund generally longer-term commercial debt. Commercial paper is not funded by deposits, and can be sponsored by a non-bank, and can involve acquiring commercial loans rather than originating commercial loans, yet the organization of the financial flows are similar to luminated banking. That is, savers extend short term loans to intermediaries, which hold commercial debt.
- (D) Securitization—Banks (and nonbanks) do not have to hold the loans that they originate. They can sell the loans to other banks (or nonbanks). If the loans are then funded by issuing securities, typically passing through the loan repayments, it is said to be securitization. The third row in **Figure 1** illustrates securitization by a bank. Securitization by banks differs from luminated banking primarily in the way that intermediaries interact with borrowers, rather than savers (although the fact that intermediaries in securitization don't hold the loans can have important indirect effects on savers). Securitization can also facilitate lending by nonbanks.[11]
- (E) Money Market Mutual Funds—MMFs gather funds from investors in order to buy relatively low risk short-term debt in securities markets. MMFS are not depicted in **Figure 1**, and the description appears to differ from laminated banking in every respect. The MMF has investors, not depositors. The MMF does not have a bank charter. The MMF generally buys debt in securities markets, rather than hold debts that it originated itself. Yet, MMFs perform financial intermediation services that are very similar to luminated banks. On the lefthand side of financial intermediation, investor withdrawals from MMFs can be very similar to depositor withdrawals from banks. On the righthand side of financial intermediation, the effect of loan defaults on an MMF has some similarities to the effect of loan defaults on a bank that holds its own loans.

There are several "banking" charters in the United States, and the definition of luminated banking used above includes these firms as well. Credit unions and thrifts also accept insured deposits, have special charters which subject them to bank-like regulation, screen applicants, offer loans, and hold loans.[12] The term insured depository institution (IDI), which can include banks, credit unions, and thrifts, is sometimes used in the same manner that the term banking is used in discussions about shadow banking. IDIs can focus solely on simple banking, but they might also participate in some shadow banking activities, such as repurchase agreements or selling the loans they originate. When this report uses the term simple banking, IDIs are considered to satisfy the requirement for a banking charter.

Brief Description of Shadow Banking

If luminated banking is limited to the four elements of simple banking described above, then the United States has always had a shadow banking sector. In a large but perhaps analytically trivial example, the borrowing of the U.S. Treasury is almost entirely conducted through shadow banking. Or, at least, Treasury is not funded through *luminated banking*—chartered banks do not screen and qualify Treasury for loans funded by deposits, and with the intention of being held by the originating institution. Rather, loans to Treasury take the form of bonds originated through securities markets, with the intention of being marketable.[13] Some Treasury securities are ultimately held by chartered banks, but even those securities were not originated by that bank.

The exact size and growth of the shadow banking sector is sensitive to the definition of "simple banking." If shadow banking is being contrasted with deposit-funded banking, then shadow banking has historically been responsible for funding most of the debt outstanding in the United States. However, the share of total debt funded by deposits at commercial banks fell from slightly over 30% in 1975 to just over 13% in 2005, and then began rising after the financial crisis. **Figure 2** shows that deposits at commercial banks are now more than 16% of total debt in the United States. To the extent that shadow banking is being used to describe alternatives to debt funded by deposits, **Figure 2** is consistent with the view that the share of the luminated banking sector dropped by nearly half after 1975, but began rising after the mortgage crisis.

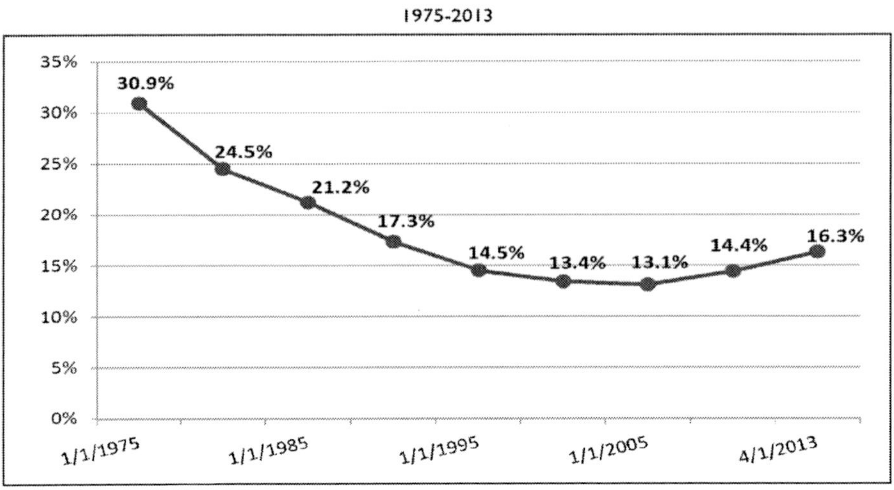

Source: Federal Reserve Economic Database.

Notes: Based on levels on January 1st of each year, on April 1st for 2013 (most recent consistent date).

Figure 2. Deposits as a Share of Total Debt in the United States.

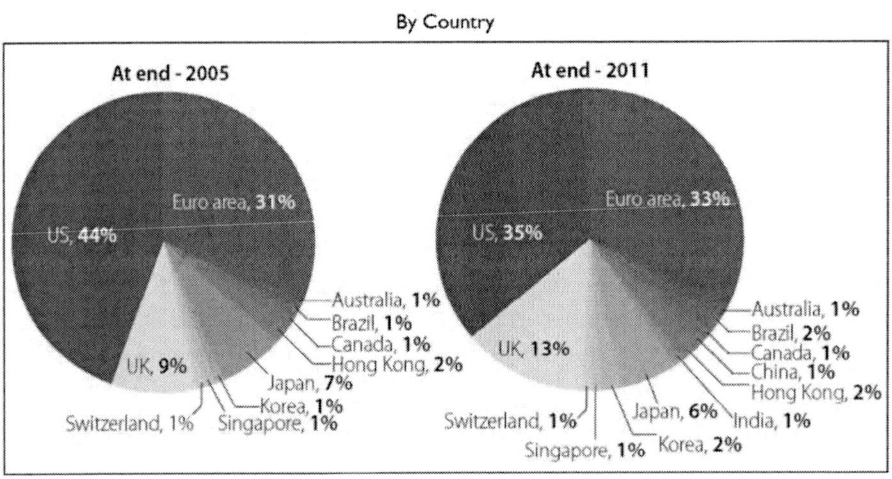

Source: Financial Stability Board.

Notes: The definition and regulation of banks varies among countries so these charts can only be estimates. These pie charts are based upon an institution-based definition of shadow banking (excluding assets held by banks even if originated through shadow banking activities such as securitization or repo agreements).

Figure 3. Share of Global Nonbank Financial Assets.

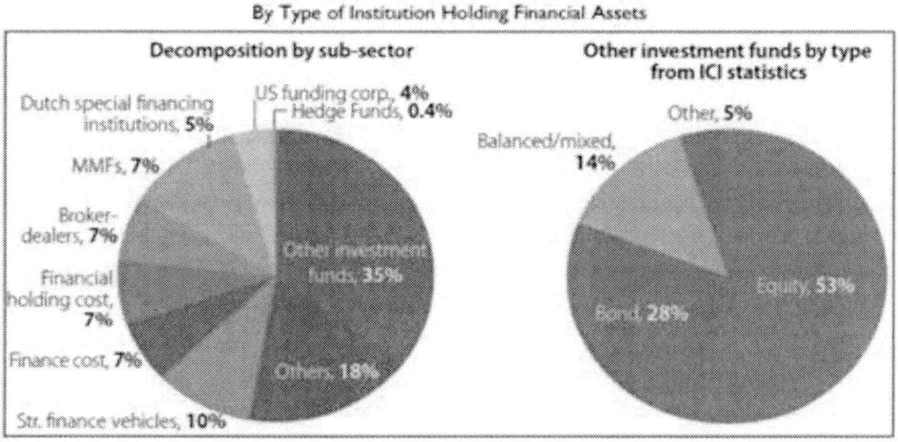

Source: Financial Stability Board.

Notes: These pie charts are based upon an institution-based definition of shadow banking (excluding assets held by banks even if originated through shadow banking activities such as securitization or repo agreements).

Figure 4. Components of Global Shadow Banking System.

Shadow banking is a global phenomenon. Because the range of permissible activities of chartered banks varies considerably across countries, the relative size of shadow banking sectors also varies considerably across countries. Because many financial markets are global, potential instability of shadow banking sectors has drawn the attention of policymakers in many countries. Shadow banking in the United States is of particular importance to international institutions such as the International Monetary Fund (IMF), Financial Stability Board (FSB), and Bank for International Settlements (BIS), because the United States financial system holds the largest single share of global nonbank assets. According to a study done by the FSB, the U.S. accounted for 44% of total world nonbank financial assets at the end of 2005 (See **Figure 3**).[14] The relative decline in the U.S. shadow banking sector, partly due to the severity of financial crisis in the U.S. shadow banking system, can be seen in that the relative share of the U.S. shadow banking institutions had declined to 35% of world nonbank assets. Note, the definition of shadow banking in these pie charts is assets held by nonbanks, and thus excludes several shadow banking activities conducted in part by chartered banks.

The FSB study reinforces the observation that it is hard to generalize about the organizational structure of shadow banking, or its regulation.

The FSB study also attempted to provide a measure of the composition of global nonbank assets by institution type, rather than by country. **Figure 4** shows that there is a wide variety of nonbank organizations that perform financial intermediation.[15] Structured finance vehicles (an element of many securitizations) accounted for 10% of the assets held by nonbanks, while money market funds accounted for 7%. Other investment funds, including bond and equity funds, held a combined 35% of global financial assets.

The shadow banking sector may exist in the United States for historical or institutional reasons. Historically, the United States had impediments to the geographic reach of chartered banks, and the scope of services they could offer.[16] For example, during industrialization, it was not always easy for chartered banks to open branches in multiple states (limited deposit taking), and during some periods of time U.S. banks had restrictions on the interest they could pay depositors.[17] Perhaps in response to regulatory restrictions on banks, financial markets evolved in the United States to aggregate funds through securities markets to assist large industrial enterprises, such as railroads and factories.[18] Similarly, savings associations in the eastern United States could and did buy whole loans originated by western financial institutions; in addition to holding loans that they originated themselves. Furthermore, during the 19th century, classes of marketable securities called debentures were issued by trusts and sold to eastern investors (and others), with the proceeds used to buy and hold mortgages originated in the west.[19] In summary, the United States has a long tradition of funding debt (including mortgage debt) through securities markets; in addition to luminated banking.

POTENTIAL POLICY PROBLEMS IN FINANCIAL INTERMEDIATION

It is difficult to generalize about the policy problems of shadow banking because the same term is used to describe firms or activities that focus on different bank-like functions. This section reviews several fundamental economic vulnerabilities in financial intermediation, and provides examples of how similar problems can exist in sectors of shadow banking.[20] This is not an exhaustive list.

Credit Risk

Recall that luminated banks accept deposits in order to fund loans held by the bank. This basic business model has a number of vulnerabilities. One vulnerability is the risk that the borrowers that the luminated bank lent to will not repay their loans (credit risk), rendering it difficult or impossible for the luminated bank to honor its obligations to its depositors. If the value of a bank's assets (the loans it holds) drops below its liabilities (to depositors) the bank has a solvency problem.

Like a luminated bank, a shadow bank that holds loans is vulnerable to credit risk. During the 2007-2009 mortgage crisis, rising mortgage defaults reduced the value of mortgage-backed securities (MBS) and whole mortgage loans held by banks and shadow banks. These losses associated with MBS and other mortgage-related securities and derivatives brought the solvency of many financial institutions into question, reducing the willingness of financial institutions to lend to each other. Realized credit risk (mortgage defaults) reduced financial institution solvency, which in turn reduced liquidity.[21] Examples of firms with reduced solvency due to credit losses include the failure of the bank (thrift) IndyMac, and the conservatorship of Fannie Mae and Freddie Mac, two mortgage securitization firms who could be considered shadow banks.[22]

Interest Rate Risk

A second problem that a luminated bank might face is interest rate risk related to its maturity mismatch. Maturity mismatch refers to the difference in length of time (term) of repayment of money borrowed compared to money lent. One way a luminated bank makes money is that the interest rate it pays to its deposits (short-term loans) is usually less than the interest rate it receives on the loans it offers (typically longer term). However, if all interest rates rise, then the simple bank may have to pay higher interest to keep its deposits, but continue to receive the lower interest rate on the longer-term loans that it still holds from the earlier time period. Paying out higher interest rates than those received is not sustainable. Furthermore, the market value of existing fixed rate bonds (the assets the bank holds) falls when interest rates rise (causing a capital loss). An example of mortgage-related interest rate risk occurred in the late 1970s and early 1980s. A 1982 Brookings publication estimated the accumulated capital loss of the mortgage portfolios of thrifts in mid-year 1981 to be $111.2 billion.[23]

Like luminated banks, shadow banks that fund themselves with short-term obligations (albeit not deposits) in order to fund longer term assets have a maturity mismatch and are also vulnerable to interest rate risk. Interest rate risk during the 2007-2009 mortgage crisis is more difficult to assess, because policy rates targeted by the Federal Reserve and rates on safe assets (like U.S. Treasury bonds) were falling, but the spread between these rates and the rate paid by many private firms widened.[24] However, even if interest rate risk was not the primary contributor to the 2007-2009 mortgage crisis, shadow banks with a maturity mismatch are still vulnerable to similar problems that plagued the savings and loans during the 1970s and 1980s.

Liquidity and Runs

A third problem a luminated bank might have is the ability to maintain liquidity. Even if all loans are fully repaid (no credit risk) and interest rates remain stable (no interest rate risk), simple banks are still vulnerable to the possibility that too many of their depositors will wish to withdraw their funds at the same time (sometimes called a "run"). Even though the bank's assets in this example are objectively sound, it might not have time to convert the loans it holds to cash to cover withdrawals. That is, the depositor withdrawals create a need for cash (the most liquid asset), but the bank's own assets take more time to convert to cash (are less liquid). For example, objectively, there may be no reason to discount the value of an auto loan or mortgage held by the bank, but if it tries to sell it in a hurry, potential buyers may not have time to evaluate and verify the quality of the auto loan or mortgage. As a result, the bank might have to sell the auto loan or mortgage at a discount.

Like a simple bank, shadow banking activities can have liquidity problems. For example, during the 2007-2009 mortgage crisis, especially in the second half of 2007, uncertainty surrounding the condition of the mortgage market caused several asset classes in shadow banking to become less liquid (more difficult to sell without suffering a severe discount). Potential investors began to reduce their exposure to financial institutions (both banks and nonbanks) that were believed to hold assets that were becoming less liquid, making it more difficult for these firms to continue to fund the illiquid assets. Some analysts, such as Gary Gorton, have described the sharp reduction in non-deposit liabilities of financial institutions in September 2008 as a *nonbank run*.[25]

Asymmetric Information

In many financial transactions, the two parties do not have the same information, a characteristic known as information asymmetry. Several categories of financial vulnerabilities are potentially related to, or magnified by, information asymmetries. For example, before the creation of the FDIC, bank runs could occur if depositors heard damaging rumors about their bank, but could not confirm the true quality of their bank's assets.[26] The potential problem of information asymmetries is more general than bank runs; for example, asymmetries can affect the ability of banks to screen loan applicants.

Information asymmetries are of particular importance to those categories of shadow banking that rely on securities markets to perform bank-like functions. For example, if a financial intermediary has several classes of assets, but needs to quickly raise cash, does the intermediary have an incentive to sell its "lemons", that is, keep its "good assets" while it sells those assets whose value has declined, but whose quality cannot be easily verified? Even if intermediaries don't actually follow this strategy, potential buyers might fear that the strategy will be followed—and discount the value of all similar securities offered for sale. For example, during the mortgage-related financial crisis of 2007-2009, private issuance of mortgage-related securities approached zero at the height of the financial crisis, even though more than 90% of mortgage borrowers did not default on their mortgages.[27]

Collateral Fire Sales

A fourth problem faced by luminated banks is related to the collateral for some of their loans. Collateral refers to an asset a borrower surrenders to the lender if the borrower fails to repay a loan. Examples of collateralized bank lending include auto loans and residential mortgages, in which the car or property being purchased by the borrower serves as collateral for the loan. Some other types of lending, like credit cards, typically are not collateralized. When an asset being purchased also serves as collateral for the loan used to finance it, lenders are vulnerable to fluctuations in the price of the collateral. Although rising house prices insulate mortgage lenders from borrower defaults, declining house prices can cause self-reinforcing fire sales. That is, during periods of declining prices, borrower defaults will result in more houses being seized as collateral for the loans, and offered at foreclosure sales. These distress sales may reinforce the decline in house prices, and contribute to even more borrower defaults and additional distress sales.

Shadow banking that relies on collateral can also be subject to self-reinforcing fire sales. For example, during the mortgage crisis of 2007-2009, some forms of ABCP were collateralized by the mortgage-backed securities that they funded. Rising mortgage defaults increased losses among for the MBS. Accounting rules and capital requirements could affect the ability of certain financial institutions to continue to fund affected MBS or attempt to raise capital.[28] As a result, some firms might choose to sell their MBS at fire sale prices, rather than try to adjust their capital or adapt in other ways. The fire sales could reinforce price declines in MBS.

Systemic Concerns

The vulnerabilities of financial intermediation described above have been framed in the context of a single institution or market. However, one definition of systemic risk is the potential for the financial system itself to spread and magnify the losses of a single institution to the wider economy.[29] For example, financial intermediaries (both banks and nonbanks) can borrow from each other, not just from depositors, investors, or other counterparties. If financial intermediaries rely too heavily on their ability to borrow from each other should financial conditions worsen, then the resilience of the system as a whole may decline. That is, each institution in isolation might maintain too small level of a cushion against credit losses, or take too few precautions against interest rate risk, or reserve too small a proportion of liquid assets, or maintain too high a proportion of loans backed by a single class of collateral, compared to the precautions that would be appropriate if they took into account the tendency of the system as a whole to magnify losses. Thus, if financial intermediaries rely on their ability to borrow should they suffer unexpectedly high defaults (credit risk), they might not sufficiently take into account the rising cost of liquid assets and maintaining solvency during times when many financial firms need to acquire additional funding at the same time.

Systemic concerns in simple banking also apply to shadow banking. In the above example, if shadow banks suffer unexpectedly high defaults (credit risk), they may all try to increase their liquidity and raise new capital (to restore their solvency) at the same time. However, each firm's planning during the "good times" may have overestimated the availability and affordability of raising additional capital, and of acquiring and maintaining liquid assets, during "bad times", when many other financial intermediaries also need additional liquidity and capital. If so, then during bad times, interbank lending may decline significantly, or interest rates on interbank loans may rise substantially, exactly at the time that many financial intermediaries seek additional financing.

REGULATION AND OTHER POLICY RESPONSES TO FINANCIAL VULNERABILITIES

Because the term shadow banking is used to describe such a diversity of firms and practices, it would be incorrect to categorize luminated banking as regulated and shadow banking as unregulated.[30] However, in many cases (but not all), the kind of regulation applied to shadow banking activities is fundamentally different than banking regulation.[31] Banking regulation is typically risk based, and typically takes into account the linkages between banks through the payment system and the interbank lending market. Securities regulation, which several categories of shadow banking involves, generally requires disclosure of material risks, but typically does not limit the risk that sophisticated securities market participants may take. This section will briefly summarize four fundamental elements (not exhaustive) of banking regulation, because several reform proposals for shadow banking can be thought of as attempting to apply the principles of banking regulation to nonbank financial intermediaries or activities.[32]

Earlier sections of this report described economic vulnerabilities of the simple banking approach. Most of these vulnerabilities also apply to shadow banking; therefore, it may be useful to review general policy intended to stabilize luminated banking before discussing policy reform proposals intended to stabilize specific shadow banking sectors.

Safety and Soundness Regulation

Bank regulators have authority to promulgate and enforce regulations to limit the risks that chartered banks take. Recall that two of the fundamental problems of financial intermediation were credit risk (the risk that loan assets would default) and interest rate risk (the risk that differences in interest rates for assets and liabilities could threaten the institution). Within its statutory framework, safety and soundness regulation includes the ability to examine the bank's assets and liabilities prior to any particular sign of financial trouble.[33] Thus, bank examiners can attempt to look for potential problems in the firm's assets or liabilities (or assets compared to liabilities). They also have the potential ability to limit the total risk that any given institution has to any single counterparty, or to limit the aggregate exposure of the chartered banking system as a whole to any single asset class (such as real estate). In the extreme, a banking regulator can revoke a firm's charter.[34] One general policy proposal for shadow banking is to apply safety and soundness regulation to nonbank financial intermediaries, if they are not already subject to analogous regulation.

Capital Requirements

Capital requirements are a subset of safety and soundness regulation. In this context, capital refers to the equity stake, or similar investment, of the investors in the bank; in general, this equity stake can absorb losses before the financial interests of depositors and other creditors of the bank are threatened.[35] Recall that credit risk was one of the fundamental problems of financial intermediation. Capital requirements can establish a minimum level of resiliency in the banking system—the ability to absorb loan losses before the institution becomes insolvent. Furthermore, if capital requirements are risk-based, they can provide incentives to limit the risk of the assets held by covered institutions. Because capital is not free, an institution subject to risk-based capital requirements would tend to evaluate the relative return of two alternative loan types against the risk-based capital requirement for that loan type. Thus risk-based capital requirements can be used to direct covered institutions toward less risky asset classes. However, and also because capital is not free, higher capital requirements tend to limit the aggregate amount of assets that can be held by covered institutions. One general policy proposal in shadow banking is to apply capital requirements to nonbank intermediaries, if they are not already subject to analogous regulation.[36]

Lender of Last Resort

A lender of last resort is an institution that has the ability to provide emergency loans during times of financial instability. Recall that liquidity was one of the fundamental problems of financial intermediation. That is, even if interest rates remained stable, and borrowers did not default, intermediaries are vulnerable to excessive withdrawals because the price of their assets might suffer steep discounts if they had to be sold in a hurry. In the United States, the Federal Reserve System is a lender of last resort to member institutions, and can expand its lending authority during financial turmoil, subject to a number of statutory restrictions.[37] One common policy approach for a lender of last resort, known as the Bagehot Rule, would encourage loans to solvent institutions, but at an above market rate (penalty rate). In some cases, for example, the Federal Reserve may only lend if it receives good collateral, which insolvent firms may run out of because their liabilities are greater than their assets. However, one critique of the 2008 financial crisis is that the lender of last resort should not just lend to solvent institutions, but also lend to insolvent institutions if those institutions are interconnected to the financial system in a way that could cause wider financial instability. One general policy proposal is to extend lender of last resort eligibility to shadow banking institutions, if they are not already eligible.

Deposit Insurance

One of the fundamental problems of financial intermediation is a depositor run, which may be more likely to occur during times of financial panic. If the sources of funding for financial intermediaries disappear, either through withdrawals or through refusals to renew expiring contracts, then intermediaries may not be able to continue to fund their assets, even if there are no loan defaults and no fluctuations in interest rates. Deposit insurance provides assurance to bank depositors that they will be protected (up to a limit) if their bank fails.[38] If deposit insurance is credible, then panic-driven depositor withdrawals may be avoided. Thus, credible deposit insurance may have prevented bank runs against savings and loans during the 1980s, even though the Federal Savings and Loan Insurance Corporation (FSLIC), which provided deposit insurance for S&L depositors, did not prevent hundreds of savings and loans from failing, or the system from requiring a bailout.

SPECIFIC SECTORS OF SHADOW BANKING

The report thus far has presented an economic framework to understand the disparate institutions and markets that are gathered under the term shadow banking. Some policymakers have proposed extending the principles of bank regulation to financial intermediation that is either conducted by nonbanks, or that might be conducted by banks but funded by nondeposits. Other options include regulating activities regardless of the type of firm engaging in it,[39] or attempting to correct mispricing that may occur when financial intermediation occurs through shadow banking.[40] This section will focus on several specific elements of shadow banking that have been highlighted by the Financial Crisis Inquiry Commission (FCIC), the Financial Stability Oversight Council (FSOC), the Financial Stability Board (FSB), the Federal Reserve Board (FRB), or the International Monetary Fund (IMF). In each case, the report briefly describes the institution or market, links it to the description of financial intermediation described above, briefly discusses its experience during the financial crisis, and describes related policy concerns. These categories are neither exhaustive nor mutually exclusive.

Repurchase Agreements

Description

In the context of shadow banking, a repurchase agreement is analogous to a banking deposit. In a repurchase agreement, one party sells another party an asset (perhaps a U.S. Treasury Bond) for one price, with an agreement to repurchase the asset on a future date at another (higher) price. The difference in the prices is functionally similar to interest on a loan. The asset being traded is similar to collateral for a loan because failure of the first party to repurchase would result in the other party keeping the asset, just as if the first party had defaulted on a loan and the second party seized the asset as collateral. Sometimes a third party is hired to assist repo transactions, often providing clearing and settlement services (tri-party repos). Intermediaries (both banks and nonbanks) can borrow funds through repos instead of through insured deposits. Like deposits, if repos are set for shorter time periods than the intermediary's assets, then the intermediary will be potentially exposed to interest rate risk, maturity mismatch, etc.

There are also differences between repos and deposits. Unlike deposits, repos are not eligible for deposit insurance. Because nonbanks can use repurchase agreements, there may be substantial financial intermediation processed by firms that are not eligible for assistance from the lender of last resort in the normal course of financial affairs. Unlike deposits, repurchase agreements use an asset as collateral. Doubts about the continued value of the asset generally used as collateral can reduce the volume of repurchase agreements available to fund intermediation (analogous to depositor withdrawals). Furthermore, if there are unexpectedly high repo defaults, the asset used as collateral may be dumped on the market, causing fire sales.

Experience During the Mortgage Crisis

The repo market experienced severe stress during the financial crisis. Economist Gary Gorton has documented the equivalent of a nonbank run on firms that had relied on the repo market for short- term financing.[41] Staff at the Federal Reserve Bank of New York (FRBNY) have been assessing the vulnerability of repos to the kinds of runs that Gorton described.[42] These authors identify both a liquidity constraint (which results in vulnerability to runs) and a collateral constraint (which results in vulnerabilities to fire sales). It is difficult to isolate the contribution of the repo market to the general crisis because many other markets experienced declines in liquidity at the same time.

Policy Concerns

Repo market policy concerns can be divided into three general categories. First, some have suggested that nonbanks that rely on repo transactions to conduct financial intermediation similar to banks should be subject to safety and soundness regulations. Title I of the Dodd-Frank Act (DFA) allows for this if the firm has more than $50 billion in assets and is designated as systemically important by the FSOC. For firms so designated, the DFA requires that the standards set for systemic nonbanks be no weaker than similar standards for banks. However, the DFA does not create a safety and soundness regime for nonbanks with less than $50 billion in assets.

Second, some have called for reforming the way repos are handled when a firm fails. For example, like other qualified financial contracts (QFCs), repo contracts are exempted from the bankruptcy estate of failing nonbanks. Under bankruptcy, payments subject to the automatic stay[43] are retrieved by the bankruptcy estate, reducing the incentive of a failing firm's creditors to race to its assets (a form of run). To the extent that the automatic stay in bankruptcy reduces the incentive of a firm's creditors to run to its assets, the exemption from the automatic stay may have contributed to the nonbank run in the repo market during 2008. Under Title II of the DFA, the FDIC would be able to avoid the bankruptcy process if there was a finding of systemic risk, and Title II gives the FDIC a limited ability to address potential problems of QFCs, including repo agreements. A firm does not have to have over $50 billion in assets or have prior designation of systemic risk for Title II to apply.

Third, some have called for reform of the techniques of repo trades. For example, the New York Federal Reserve, which participates in many repo transactions, has sought to improve certain technical features of the settlement system (the "plumbing" or "back office" function).[44] Similarly, some have expressed concern that delays in clearing and settlement expose the intermediaries in tri-party repos (the 3rd party) to undue credit risk. Finally, because repos are similar to collateralized loans, some are concerned that repo defaults or settlement fails could lead to fire sales.

Nonbank Intermediaries

Description

A nonbank intermediary is a firm without a bank charter that gathers funds from savers in order to fund loans to borrowers. Nonbank intermediaries come in many forms. For example, a mortgage company such as EMC Mortgage and an investment firm (nondepository) such as Bear Stearns could partner to generate mortgages that are then packaged and sold to investors (securitization through nonbanks). Similarly, a nonbank such as Fannie Mae can sell short term bonds that it uses to fund the acquisition of longer term mortgages that it keeps in portfolio.[45] Or, in a non- securitization setting, a nonbank like MF Global can fund itself through repo transactions to acquire and hold debt issued by sovereign governments. The exact form of nonbank intermediation can vary a great deal, and the regulatory status of the firms participating can also vary a great deal. In these examples, Fannie Mae was subject to safety and soundness regulation, capital requirements, and had access to some emergency liquidity, but MF Global was not. Yet, MF Global was subject to regulation for securities that it issued to potential investors, and the way it handled customer accounts.

Experience During the Mortgage Crisis

During the mortgage crisis, many nonbank intermediaries experienced a liquidity crunch, and some failed outright. In some cases, financial turmoil prevented evaluation of the true value of complex mortgage-related securities in a timely manner, perhaps exacerbating price declines, and contributing to further fire sales. Under the normal course of events, failing nonbanks would be resolved through the bankruptcy process, in which similarly situated creditors must be treated similarly. Perhaps believing that financial instability would be magnified if certain creditors suffered losses, some policymakers wanted to avoid the bankruptcy process.[46] Policymakers responded in at least two ways. The Federal Reserve set up special lending facilities (such as TALF) to support the liquidity concerns of nonbanks that could pledge eligible collateral. The Federal Reserve created special lending facilities to avoid the bankruptcy filing of Bear Stearns and AIG (but not of Lehman Brothers). Congress enacted the Housing and Economic Recovery Act (HERA). Under HERA, the newly created Federal Housing Finance Agency (FHFA) and Treasury administered a conservatorship of the GSEs in which the returns on some GSE senior securities were curtailed, but many other GSE obligations were fully honored.

Policy Concerns

Because there are many types of nonbanks, and nonbank business models, it is difficult to generalize about this category. However, it may be useful to distinguish between policy proposals directed at activities in which banks and nonbanks both participate, and policy proposals about the eligibility of nonbanks for government efforts to address financial instability.

The DFA attempts to address the participation of nonbanks in loan originations for consumers. Title X of the DFA creates a Consumer Financial Protection Bureau (CFPB) with authority to make rules for many consumer lending transactions that apply to both banks and nonbanks.[47]

The DFA changes policy options regarding nonbanks before and after a future crisis. Before a crisis, nonbanks with more than $50 billion in assets can be subjected to safety and soundness regulation if there is a determination of systemic risk concerns under Title I. Even smaller nonbanks can be resolved by the FDIC if there is a determination that their failure could contribute to financial instability under Title II. However, Title XI of the DFA limits the ability of the Federal Reserve to provide emergency lending to a single nonbank (as it did for Bear Stearns); rather, future emergency lending facilities would have to have more general eligibility criteria.

Asset Backed Commercial Paper

Description

Commercial paper is a very old type of security in which commercial loans are funded through securities markets, even if sponsored by a chartered bank. Asset Backed Commercial Paper (ABCP) commonly refers to senior short-term debt securities that are backed by commercial loans.[48] Both banks and nonbanks can sponsor vehicles to issue ABCP; for example, a bank could create ABCP to sell its credit card loan collectibles, while an auto financing company could create ABCP to sell its auto loan repayments. Typically, the sponsor of ABCP receives a fee for administering the assets of the ABCP facility and often promises to provide emergency loans (liquidity) to the ABCP facility if other sources of funding are distressed.

Experience During the Mortgage Crisis

Part of the mortgage boom during the housing bubble was financed with ABCP.[49] Beginning in August 2007, ABCP for subprime mortgage loans found it difficult or impossible to get external financing to support continued activity. As a result, many ABCP facilities turned to their sponsors for liquidity. As a result, many began absorbing subprime assets from sponsored ABCP that had not previously been disclosed on their balance sheets. Furthermore, the value of these mortgage- related assets had to be written-down. Late 2007 and early 2008 has been referred to as a liquidity crunch, in which uncertainty about further mortgage security related write-downs created financial uncertainty and mistrust in the interbank lending market. Some of these problems led to fire sales of the mortgages and mortgage-related assets that backed ABCP. Thus, credit losses on subprime mortgages contributed to liquidity problems for bank and nonbank intermediaries. The Federal Reserve created the Term Asset Backed Loan Facility (TALF) during the financial crisis to alleviate further fire sales of ABCP assets.

Policy Concerns

Several policy changes have been implemented to attempt to address future problems in ABCP. The accounting profession has attempted to address some of the uncertainty issues by revising the way contingent liabilities (such as ABCP liquidity sponsorship) are reported in accounting statements. For example, FAS 166 and 167 have amended FAS 140 to address concerns about the recording of a true sale of assets from a sponsor to its ABCP.[50] Similarly, the banking regulators have also addressed ABCP sponsorship by revising capital treatment for contingent liabilities, including promises to provide liquidity to sponsored ABCP.[51] Emergency lending facilities such as TALF have expired, but the Federal Reserve's emergency lending authority for similar general access programs is preserved under Title XI of the DFA.

Securitization

Description

Securitization is similar to ABCP in that loans are funded through securities markets. Under securitization, a trust or similar facility is created that acquires assets with a stream of payments, such as loans. The trust issues new securities under its own name that pass through the asset payments to the holders of the securities. For example, a trust could be formed that holds mortgages, with the payments by mortgage borrowers being passed through to the holders of the securities. Although this example used mortgages, any stream of payments from credit cards to toll booth collections can be securitized.[52] One feature of securitization is that the terms of the securities issued by the trust (time of scheduled payments, relative seniority to other securities issued by the trust, etc.) do not have to match the timing or interest of the assets held by the trust as long as all payments are accounted for (complete pass through except for administrative expenses, and perhaps credit support). Chartered banks can participate in securitization by selling their loans, as can nonbank lenders. Typically, securitization conducted through private label firms did not include an issuer guarantee to cover credit risk. In contrast, securitization by the government sponsored enterprises does include a guarantee for credit risk, but not for interest rate risk.[53]

Experience During the Mortgage Crisis

Most observers, including all three opinions in the FCIC report, consider aspects of securitization to have contributed to the magnitude of the financial crisis, although there are different views on how or why. All three FCIC opinions agree with the following description of events.[54] Once credit losses escalated in the mortgage market, the demand for mortgage-backed securities disappeared. Many mortgage finance companies that originated and sold mortgages to private label securitizers failed. Some issuers of private label MBS suffered large losses because they retained some credit interest in the securities they sold (in some cases by retaining junior tranches to improve the credit rating of other tranches and in other cases by offering other contingent liabilities). Banks and other firms owned private label MBS, and had overestimated the relative safety of MBS. Firms that provided insurance to MBS securitization, or securities with similar functions, failed (this includes the monoline insurers and AIG). Fannie Mae and Freddie Mac, which had to cover the credit losses of the mortgages they securitized, were placed in government conservatorship, with contracts with Treasury to assure their financial condition. Legal challenges to the servicing of securitized mortgages by defaulting homeowners delayed resolution of foreclosed homes, potentially extending the time period of surplus distressed homes in geographic areas with the highest concentration of mortgage defaults.

Policy Concerns

Many changes have been made to private-label and GSE securitization since the beginning of financial turmoil in August 2007. In July 2008, HERA created a new regulator for Fannie Mae and Freddie Mac. In September, 2008, these two GSEs were placed in conservatorship. However, the final disposition of the mortgage GSEs has not yet been determined.[55]

The volume of private label securitization is still extremely low compared to before the financial turmoil began. The Dodd-Frank Act created a new regulatory framework for the securitization process, especially for residential mortgage securitization. Under Title IX of the act, a new office was created within the SEC to regulate nationally recognized credit rating organizations (NRCRO), which are the firms that provide a label for the relative risk of marketable securities. Under Title VII, financial derivatives that were used to help construct complex securitized products must be standardized and cleared on an organized exchange regulated by the CFTC (or SEC), if possible. Under Title IX, firms that sponsor securitizations must retain a portion of the risk of the securities issued. Financial regulators issue rules for retained risk for each asset class, including for mortgages (QRM Rule). Under Title XIV, mortgages must meet certain standards to be assured certain legal protections in the case of default (QM rule), including securitized mortgages. Under Title X, most consumer financial products that are securitized, including credit cards, mortgages, and student loans, will be regulated for consumer protection by a single agency, the CFPB.

Some policies have yet to be fully specified and implemented. Some industry participants believe that the volume of securitization, especially for mortgages, will remain low until regulatory uncertainty is addressed. For example, mortgage securitizers would like to see the standards for the QM rule and the QRM rule be consistent, but differing legal contexts for the primary market (mortgage origination) and some secondary markets (securities regulation) may make such consistency problematic even if regulators use identical language in the two rules. Another potential concern is the creation and maintenance of a national mortgage database, which some analysts believe could address some of the uncertainty about the contents of MBS during the period of financial turmoil, and the legal challenges to the securitization process that escalated when the foreclosure volume increased.

Money Market Funds

Description

The SEC describes money market funds (MMFs) as "a type of mutual fund that is required by law to invest in low-risk securities."[56] MMFs raise their funds by selling shares, which are technically not deposits and are not insured. MMFs hold short-term debt in the form of government securities, certificates of deposit, commercial paper of highly rated companies, or other low-risk and highly liquid securities. MMFs can be structured to allow investors to redeem their shares (open ended MMF), or not (closed end). The difference between the value of an MMF's assets and its liabilities is called the Net Asset Value, or NAV. Since investors would like to receive more than a dollar for every dollar invested, MMFs attempt to keep their NAV greater than $1.00. If the NAV falls below $1.00, the MMF has "broken the buck," and its investors are essentially receiving negative interest on their shares.

Experience During the Mortgage Crisis

The MMF industry suffered a run after the failure of Lehman Brothers in September, 2008. Recall that in **Figure 1**, an open end MMF has structurally similar financial intermediation as a depository bank. Lehman's bankruptcy filing meant that holders of its debt would likely receive less than full payment of the debt (credit risk). As a result, a prominent MMF (the Reserve Fund) that held Lehman's debt announced that it had "broken the buck." The Reserve Fund's announcement, combined with more general financial turmoil, led investors to withdraw their shares from MMFs, which open end funds could not avoid. People who had relied on MMFs to finance their activities, such as governments and issuers of commercial paper, lost their traditional source of funding.

Policymakers undertook emergency measures to try to stabilize the MMFs following the run on the industry. Treasury announced an insurance plan for

MMFs, backed by the exchange stabilization fund (ESF)—a fund available to Treasury to stabilize the dollar under the old Bretton Woods exchange rate system. Subsequently, Congress enacted legislation to prohibit Treasury from using the ESF to stabilize MMFs in the future.[57] However, the extension of government assistance for one asset class during a crisis may create an expectation of assistance should a future crisis occur, perhaps encouraging excessive risk taking (moral hazard).[58]

Policy Concerns

MMFs continue to face the risk of runs. Structurally, the industry faces possible credit risk, maturity mismatch, liquidity problems, and other fundamental problems of financial intermediation. Prior to the financial crisis, the regulatory approach of the SEC had been to treat MMFs as securities issuers. Although eligible assets of MMFs are limited, and the portfolios of MMFs are subject to diversity requirements, MMFs are not subject to periodic examinations in the way that banks are. Rather, MMFs are required to provide periodic disclosures like other firms funded through securities markets. The experience of the crisis has led other financial regulators to encourage the SEC to adopt a prudential regulatory approach, more similar to banking, than the traditional securities regulation for MMFs. Through the minutes of the FSOC, other regulators have formally expressed their desire for additional regulations to address the potential for runs.

The SEC proposed several new rules for MMFs on June 5, 2013.[59] The formal comment period ended in September 2013, but final rules had not been issued as of time of this report's publication. The proposed rule contained two primary features designed to avoid runs in the MMF industry. The first would require a floating net asset value (NAV) for prime institutional money market funds. The second would allow the use of liquidity fees and redemption gates in times of stress. Redemption gates include provisions that limit the ability of investors to fully withdraw their funds in a crisis, such as temporary fees or aggregate withdrawal limits. The call for comment included discussion of allowing these as alternatives or to be used in combination. In addition to these primary features, proposed rule also included additional diversification and disclosure measures that would apply under either alternative.

CONCLUSION

Although researchers use the term shadow banking inconsistently, with important implications for their policy analysis, the concept always excludes luminated banking. The term laminated banking describes debt funded by the insured deposits of firms with special banking charters. Nonbanks often facilitate shadow banking by funding debt through securities markets. Similarly, banks can be involved in shadow banking if they find short-term substitutes for insured deposits. Whether offered by nonbanks or by banks, the creation and funding of debt is often subject to several economic vulnerabilities linked to financial intermediation, such as vulnerabilities to runs or fire-sales.

Securities markets and firms with banking charters are both regulated; thus, much of what is described as shadow banking is subject to some federal regulation. However, the type of regulation that applies to shadow banking varies. Banking regulation is typically prudential (risk- based), but securities regulation typically is not. Securities regulation is typically not limited to firms with a special charter, but banking regulation typically is. Bank holding companies that participate in shadow banking are subject to prudential regulation, at least on a consolidated level.

The FSOC and the FSB have identified several components of shadow banking that may be of heightened concern. The diversity of these practices and firms makes broad generalizations about policies to address shadow banking difficult. In many cases, policy proposals attempt to apply bank-like regulation to nonbanks. The Dodd-Frank Act extends several prudential regulatory principles associated with banking regulation to nonbanks if they are designated as systemically important. Some believe that extension of bank-like regulation is inappropriate for some firms with different balance sheets (such as insurance companies). Others believe that the Dodd-Frank Act did not extend bank-like regulation enough because some intermediaries are too small to be systemically important, but the industry as a whole may be financially vulnerable (such as MMFs).

End Notes

[1] For example, the head of the FDIC emphasized the leverage of non-bank affiliates and off-balance sheet entities in testimony to Congress regarding the causes of the financial crisis. "Statement of Sheila C. Bair, Chairman, Federal Deposit Insurance Corporation on FDIC Oversight: Examining and Evaluating the Role of the Regulator during the Financial Crisis

and Today," House Subcommittee on Financial Institutions and Consumer Credit, May 26, 2011, available at http://www.fdic.gov/news/news/speeches/chairman/spmay2611.html.

[2] There is no single authoritative definition of shadow banking. Even in the speech in which this quote is taken, Federal Reserve Governor Tarullo later suggests that being considered a "safe asset" is also an essential feature of shadow banking. This report will use Governor Tarullo's more generic definition rather than "safety" in order to encompass several practices that Congress has included under the rubric of shadow banking during hearings and other deliberations. The quote is taken from Governor Daniel K. Tarullo, "Speech before the Federal Reserve Bank of San Francisco Conference on Challenges in Global Finance: The Role of Asia," June 12, 2012, available at http://www.federalreserve.gov/newsevents/speech/tarullo20120612a.htm.

[3] *Financial Crisis Inquiry Report* (Majority Opinion), Financial Crisis Inquiry Commission, U.S. Government Printing Office, pp. 27-37, available at http://bookstore.gpo.gov.

[4] For example, member agencies of the Financial Stability Board (FSB) have issued recommendations for coordinated regulatory changes for several shadow banking practices. See "An Overview of Policy Recommendations for Shadow Banking," Financial Stability Board, 29 August 2013, available at http://www.financialstabilityboard.org/publications/r_130829a.htm.

[5] This report focuses on regulatory differences between banking and shadow banking, not on implications for monetary policy. For a discussion of the role of shadow banking in monetary innovation, especially in the supply of collateral for financial transactions, see Singh, Manmohan, "The Economics of Shadow Banking," prepared for the Reserve Bank of Australia Conference on Liquidity and Funding Markets, Aug., 2013, available at http://www.rba.gov.au/publications/ confs/2013/pdf/singh.pdf.

[6] Each of the chosen sectors has been discussed in recent congressional deliberations in the context of shadow banking. It is not an exhaustive list of topics that could fit a definition of shadow banking.

[7] One financial industry primer included a table of six differing definitions of shadow banking offered by the chairman of the Federal Reserve, agency research staff, academics, and the Financial Stability Board. Some of the definitions sought to exclude chartered banks, while others emphasized the participation of banks in parts of the shadow banking system. See Exhibit 1 of "The Deloitte Shadow Banking Index", Deloitte Center for Financial Services, available at http://www.deloitte.com/assets/Dcom-UnitedStates/Local%20Assets/Documents/CFO_Center_FT/ US_FSI_The_Deloitte_Shadow_Banking_052912.pdf.

[8] IMF research economists have critiqued definitions of shadow banking that attempt to exclude banks. " ... , many shadow banking activities, for instance, liquidity puts to securitisation structured investment vehicles, collateral operations of dealer banks, repos, and so on, operate within banks, especially systemic ones." Stijn Claessens and Lev Ratnovski, "What is Shadow Banking?" Vox.edu, 23 August 2013, available at http://www.voxeu.org/article/what- shadow-banking.

[9] For example, a staff research paper of the Federal Reserve Bank of New York would limit shadow banking only to situations in which participants do not have an explicit public backstop. Yet, as shown in prior footnotes, the chair of the FDIC, the Financial Stability Board, Federal Reserve governors, and research staff of the IMF, have all expressed concern regarding the connection between banks and shadow banking practices, even if those practices are technically off balance sheet. See "Shadow Banking: A Review of the Literature," Tobias Adrian and Adam Ashcraft, FRBNY working paper no. 580, October 2012, available at http://www.newyorkfed.org/research/staff_reports/sr580.html.

[10] CRS Report R43087, *Who Regulates Whom and How? An Overview of U.S. Financial Regulatory Policy for Banking and Securities Markets*, by Edward V. Murphy.

[11] CRS Report RS22722, *Securitization and Federal Regulation of Mortgages for Safety and Soundness*, by Edward V. Murphy.

[12] CRS Report R43087, *Who Regulates Whom and How? An Overview of U.S. Financial Regulatory Policy for Banking and Securities Markets*, by Edward V. Murphy.

[13] On a smaller scale, the federal government is itself a nonbank lender through programs such as the Department of Education's direct student loan program. Furthermore, to the extent Treasury chooses to fund itself with bonds of a shorter maturity than the student loans, and U.S. assets are considered safe havens, the federal government meets the stricter criteria of some of the narrower definitions of shadow banking (maturity mismatch and assets perceived as safe money substitutes). The point is not that because the funding of the federal government meets some of the definitions of shadow banking that the federal government is a systemic concern; rather, that various forms of shadow banking are, and have been, common.

[14] "Global Shadow Banking Monitoring Report, 2012," FSB, Nov. 2012, p. 10, available at http://www.financialstabilityboard.org/publications/r_121118c.pdf.

[15] Ibid.

[16] Restrictions on interstate banking were imposed at both the state and federal level, and several of these restrictions were reduced in the late 20th century. The extent and nature of the restrictions changed over time. For an introduction to the history written in the context of deregulation of interstate banking, see "Going Interstate: A New Dawn For U.S. Banking," Michelle Clark Neely, Regional Economist, July. 1994, Federal Reserve Bank of St. Louis, available at http://www.stlouisfed.org/publications/re/articles/?id=1885.

[17] A description of some of these restrictions and their removal over time is included in "The Real Effects of Banking Deregulation," Philip Strahan, Nov. 2002, available at http://research. stlouisfed.org/conferences/policyconf/papers/ Strahan.pdf.

[18] An international comparison of financial system development is found in "Economic, Political, and Legal Factors in Financial System Development," Caroline Fohlin, Social Science Working Paper 1089, May 2002. Specific reference to the effects of bank regulations in United States can be found on page 7, available at http://www.hss.caltech.edu/SSPapers/wp1089.pdf.

[19] Snowden, Kenneth "Covered Farm Mortgage Bonds in the Nineteenth Century," NBER 16462, available at http://www.econ.ucla.edu/workshops/papers/History/Snowden%20w16242.pdf.

[20] More detailed comparisons of policy problems and responses in banking and securities markets can be found in Allen, Franklin and Richard Herring, "Banking Regulation versus Securities Market Regulation," Wharton working paper 01-29, July 2001, available at http://finance. wharton.upenn.edu/~allenf/download/Vita/0129.pdf.

[21] CRS Report RL34182, *Financial Crisis? The Liquidity Crunch of August 2007*, by Darryl E. Getter et al.

[22] Analysts that exclude institutions with a federal backstop (even if implicit) from the definition of shadow banking would not consider Fannie Mae and Freddie Mac shadow banks. However, if such a definition is used, then many sectors in which chartered banks participate should not be considered shadow banking.

[23] Carron, Andrew, *The Plight of the Thrift Institutions*, Brookings, 1981, p. 18.

[24] "Reflections on a Year in Crisis," speech by Federal Reserve Chairman Ben Bernanke at the Federal Reserve Bank of Kansas City's Annual Economic Symposium, Jackson Hole, Wyoming, Aug, 2009, available at http://www.federalreserve.gov/newsevents/speech/bernanke20090821a.htm.

[25] Gorton, Gary "Slapped in the Face by the Invisible Hand," prepared for the FRB Atlanta conference on financial markets, May 2009, available at http://www.frbatlanta.org/news/conferen/09fmc/gorton.pdf.

[26] Calomiris, Charles W. and Gary Gorton. "The Origins of Banking Panics: Models, Facts, and Bank Regulation." In *Financial Markets and Financial Crises*, edited by R. Glenn Hubbard, 109-173. Chicago: University of Chicago Press, 1991.

[27] Data for historical issuance of residential mortgage backed securities (RMBS) can be found on the Securities Industry and Financial markets Association (SIFMA) website, http://www.sifma.org/research/statistics.aspx.

[28] Merrill, Craig B., Taylor D. Nadauld, René M. Stulz, and Shane M. Sherlund, "Why did financial institutions sell RMBS at fire sale prices during the financial crisis?" Wharton Working Paper 13-06, February 2012, available at http://fic.wharton.upenn.edu/fic/papers/13/13-06.pdf.

[29] CRS Report R42083, *Financial Stability Oversight Council: A Framework to Mitigate Systemic Risk*, by Edward V. Murphy.

[30] Unless one defines shadow banking to exclude regulated firms. However, because securities markets are regulated, very few of the firms and activities that are called shadow banking would meet such a definition.

[31] CRS Report R43087, *Who Regulates Whom and How? An Overview of U.S. Financial Regulatory Policy for Banking and Securities Markets*, by Edward V. Murphy.

[32] This discussion is not necessarily an endorsement of banking regulation as superior to securities regulation. Savings and loans were subject to prudential regulation, had deposit insurance, and had access to a lender of last resort, yet savings and loans experienced a crisis.

[33] FDIC, "Risk Management Manual of Examination Policies," available at http://www.fdic.gov/regulations/safety/manual/section3-2.html.

[34] But the existence of multiple charters that permit similar banking services may allow firms to avoid regulators with a reputation for revoking charters or onerous supervision. This is called regulatory arbitrage.

[35] CRS Report R42744, U.S. *Implementation of the Basel Capital Regulatory Framework*, by Darryl E. Getter.

[36] Fannie Mae and Freddie Mac are examples of firms that perform maturity transformation similar to banks, but without a bank charter. Both institutions are subject to safety and soundness regulation and minimum capital requirements.

[37] CRS Report RL34427, *Financial Turmoil: Federal Reserve Policy Responses*, by Marc Labonte.

[38] CRS Report R41718, *Federal Deposit Insurance for Banks and Credit Unions*, by Darryl E. Getter.

[39] Activity-based regulation could be applied to both banks and non-banks. Examples of this approach might include the Truth in Lending Act (TILA), which required disclosures for many consumer loans and applies to both banks and non-banks. The powers of the Consumer Financial Protection Bureau can apply to both banks and nonbanks.

[40] If participants in a shadow banking transaction are believed not to take into account the full social costs (including risk of financial instability), then this approach would be to attempt to impose a corrective fee on the transaction. This approach is analogous to Pigovian taxes on activities believed to cause negative externalities, such as pollution.

[41] "Slapped in the Face by the Invisible Hand," Gary Gorton, prepared for the FRB Atlanta conference on financial markets, May 2009, available at http://www.frbatlanta.org/news/conferen/09fmc/gorton.pdf.

[42] "Repo Runs", Antoine Martin, David Skeie, and Ernst-Ludwig von Thadden, Federal Reserve Bank of New York Staff Reports, no. 444, April 2010; revised January 2012, available at http://www.newyorkfed.org/research/ staff_reports/sr444.pdf.

[43] The automatic stay refers to a feature of bankruptcy law in which payments by the bankrupt (including some recent payments already transmitted) are gathered in a pool awaiting coordination and distribution to creditors according to a predefined set of rules.

[44] "TriParty Repo Infrastructure Reform," White Paper Prepared by the Federal Reserve Bank of New York, May 17, 2010, available at http://www.newyorkfed.org/banking/nyfrb_triparty_whitepaper.pdf.

[45] In this example, Fannie Mae is issuing debt under its own name, not pass-through MBS, and holding the mortgages in its own portfolio.

[46] Chairman Ben S. Bernanke "Lessons from the failure of Lehman Brothers," Before the Committee on Financial Services, U.S. House of Representatives, Washington, D.C., April 20, 2010.

[47] CRS Report R42572, *The Consumer Financial Protection Bureau (CFPB): A Legal Analysis*, by David H. Carpenter.

[48] Not all commercial paper is asset-backed.

[49] Financial Crisis Inquiry Commission, Financial Crisis Inquiry Report, U.S. Government Printing Office, p. 113, available at http://bookstore.gpo.gov.

[50] Regulatory Capital Standards Final Rule Amending the Risk-Based Capital Rules to Reflect the Issuance of FAS 166 and FAS 167, FIL-3-2010, Jan. 2010, available at http://www.fdic.gov/news/news/financial/2010/fil10003.html.

[51] Ibid.

[52] Kothari, Vinod, Securitization: *The Financial Instrument of the Future*, John Wiley and Sons, Hoboken, NJ, 2006.

[53] CRS Report R40800, *GSEs and the Government's Role in Housing Finance: Issues for the 113th Congress*, by N. Eric Weiss.

[54] Financial Crisis Inquiry Report, Financial Crisis Inquiry Commission, U.S. Government Printing Office, p 113, available at bookstore.gpo.gov.

[55] CRS Report RL34623, *Housing and Economic Recovery Act of 2008*, coordinated by N. Eric Weiss.

[56] http://www.sec.gov/spotlight/money-market.shtml.

[57] The Emergency Economic Stabilization Act (EESA) in 2008 included language prohibiting the use of the gold- exchange fund to provide assistance to money market mutual funds.

[58] The regulations for MMFs already limit their assets to classes believed to be safe, which limits some forms of moral hazard.

[59] SEC, Release No. 33-9408, IA-3616; IC-30551; File No. S7-03-13, RIN 3235-AK61, Money Market Fund Reform, available at http://www.sec.gov/rules/proposed/2013/33-9408.pdf.

In: Shadow Banking ...
Editor: Vivian Kelemen

ISBN: 978-1-63117-527-5

Chapter 2

WHO REGULATES WHOM AND HOW? AN OVERVIEW OF U.S. FINANCIAL REGULATORY POLICY FOR BANKING AND SECURITIES MARKETS*

Edward V. Murphy

SUMMARY

Financial regulatory policies are of interest to Congress because firms, consumers, and governments fund many of their activities through banks and securities markets. Furthermore, financial instability can damage the broader economy. Financial regulation is intended to protect borrowers and investors that participate in financial markets and mitigate financial instability. This report provides an overview of the regulatory policies of the agencies that oversee banking and securities markets and explains which agencies are responsible for which institutions, activities, and markets. Some agencies regulate particular types of institutions for risky behavior or conflicts of interest, some agencies promulgate rules for certain financial transactions no matter what kind of institution engages in them, and other agencies enforce existing rules for some institutions, but

* This is an edited, reformatted and augmented version of a Congressional Research Service publication, CRS Report for Congress R43087, prepared for Members and Committees of Congress, from www.crs.gov, dated May 28, 2013.

not for others. These regulatory activities are not necessarily mutually exclusive.

Banking

U.S. banking regulation traditionally focuses on prudence. Banks' business decisions are regulated for safety and soundness and adequate capital. In addition, banks are given access to a lender of last resort, and some bank creditors are provided guarantees (deposit insurance). Regulating the risks that banks take is believed to help smooth the credit cycle. The credit cycle refers to periodic booms and busts in lending. Prudential safety and soundness regulation and capital requirements date back to the 1860s when bank credit formed the money supply. The Federal Reserve (Fed) as lender of last resort was created following the Panic of 1907. Deposit insurance was established in the 1930s to reduce the incentive of depositors to withdraw funds from banks during a financial panic.

Securities, Derivatives, and Similar Contract Markets

Federal securities regulation has traditionally focused on disclosure and conflicts of interest, rather than on prudence. Securities regulation is typically designed to ensure that market participants have access to enough information to make informed decisions, rather than to limit the riskiness of the business models of publicly traded firms. Firms that sell securities to the public must register with the Securities and Exchange Commission (SEC). SEC registration in no way implies that an investment is safe, only that material risks have been disclosed. The SEC also registers several classes of securities market participants and firms. It has enforcement powers for certain types of industry misstatements or omissions and for certain types of conflicts of interest. Derivatives trading is supervised by the Commodity Futures Trading Commission (CFTC), which oversees trading on the futures exchanges, which have self-regulatory responsibilities as well. The Wall Street Reform and Consumer Protection Act (Dodd-Frank Act, P.L. 111-203) required more disclosures in the over-the-counter (off-exchange) derivatives market than prior to the financial crisis and has granted the CFTC and SEC authority over large derivatives traders.

Government Sponsored Enterprises

The Federal Housing Finance Agency (FHFA) oversees a group of government-sponsored enterprises (GSEs). Two of the GSEs, Fannie Mae and Freddie Mac, securitize residential mortgages, and they were placed in conservatorship following mortgage losses in 2008. In the conservatorship, the Treasury provides financial support to the GSEs and FHFA and Treasury have managerial control over the enterprises. FHFA also regulates the Federal Home Loan Bank (FHLB) system, a GSE composed of 12 regional banks owned by the 8,000 financial institutions that they serve.

Changes Following the 2008 Financial Crisis

The Dodd-Frank Act created the interagency Financial Stability Oversight Council (FSOC) and authorized a permanent staff to monitor systemic risk and consolidated bank regulation from five agencies to four. The DFA granted the Federal Reserve oversight authority and the Federal Deposit Insurance Corporation (FDIC) resolution authority over the largest financial firms. The Dodd-Frank Act consolidated consumer protection rulemaking, which had been dispersed among several federal agencies, in the new Consumer Financial Protection Bureau.

Special Topics

The appendices in this report include additional information on topics, such as the regulatory structure prior to the Dodd-Frank Act (DFA), organizational differences among financial firms, and the rating system that regulators use to evaluate the health of banks. A list of common acronyms and a glossary of common financial terms are also included as appendices.

INTRODUCTION

Most people in the United States (and other developed nations) have rejected the Shakespearean maxim, "neither a borrower nor a lender be." Many people use loans to finance at least part of their education and job training during their youth, use mortgages to finance at least part of their home while starting a family, invest in stocks and bonds during middle age, and rely on the returns to the value of their stocks, bonds, and homes to at least partially pay for retirement during old age. Business firms, municipalities, and sovereign governments also rely on the financial system to help build the productive capital necessary for a well-functioning society and to foster economic growth. Financial regulatory policies are of interest to Congress because of the repercussions for individual constituents, the financing of firms and governments, and long-run economic growth.

This report provides a framework to help answer the question, "who regulates whom in U.S. financial markets, and how?" At the federal level, the answer often depends on first identifying both the policy problem and the proposed solution. For example, there are federal regulatory overlaps in which one agency can oversee a firm because of the firm's charter, a second agency regulates some of the activities that the firm is engaging in, but a third agency controls a government initiative to resolve or alleviate a problem related to the firm or its activities. On the other hand, there are regulatory gaps in which some of the firms participating in a financial activity do not have regulated charters, and the activity believed to be causing a problem does not have a regulator. Thus, answering "who regulates whom" requires first identifying the problem to be regulated, and how. This report provides an analysis of financial regulatory policy. It is not intended as a roadmap of legal jurisdiction; rather, it helps to match financial regulatory agencies to financial regulatory policies based on the kinds of financial difficulties that they generally address. Many of these difficulties are related to what economists call *market failures*, which can be loosely described as instances in which market prices and participants do not fully take into account all of the costs and benefits of their actions.

Table 1 presents a list of financial regulators. In the United States, it may be useful to distinguish between regulators that generally focus on *prudence* (i.e., monitoring and regulating the risks that a specific firm engages in) and regulators that generally focus on *disclosure* (i.e., monitoring and regulating the information that firms and exchanges provide to potential market participants).

Table 1. Federal Financial Regulators and Organizations (acronyms and area of authority)

Prudential Bank Regulators	Securities and Derivatives Regulators	Other Regulators of Financial Activities	Coordinating Forum
Office of the Comptroller of the Currency (OCC)	Securities and Exchange Commission (SEC)	Federal Housing Finance Agency (FHFA)	Financial Stability Oversight Council (FSOC)
Federal Deposit Insurance	Commodities Futures	Consumer Financial	Federal Financial
Corporation (FDIC)	Trading Commission (CFTC)	Protection Bureau (CFPB)	Institutions Examinations Council (FFIEC)
National Credit Union Administration (NCUA)			President's Working Group on Capital Markets (PWG)
Federal Reserve Board(FRB, or the Fed)			

Source: The Congressional Research Service (CRS).

Four federal agencies have prudential authority to examine banks, thrifts, and credit unions.[1] Two agencies oversee markets for financial contracts (securities and derivatives). The agencies listed in the "other" category regulate housing government-sponsored enterprises (GSEs) and consumer financial products, respectively. The entities listed in the coordinating forum category are made up of the other financial regulators with related duties or functions and facilitate communication and coordination among member agencies. Two agencies either regulate an activity regardless of the type of institution that engages in it or provide prudential regulation to nonbanks.[2] The agencies are discussed in more detail below.

The policy problems and regulatory approaches of the agencies listed in *Table 1* vary considerably. Before providing a detailed analysis of each agency, it may be useful to consider how the agencies are related to each other and briefly sketch the types of policies they generally pursue. The prudential bank regulators and the Federal Housing Finance Agency (FHFA) examine firms with specific charters and monitor and limit the risks that their chartered firms engage in. Securities and derivatives regulators monitor exchanges that host the trading of financial contracts, oversee the disclosures that market participants provide, and enforce rules against deceptive or manipulative trading practices. Unlike prudential bank regulators, securities regulators generally do not monitor the composition of assets and liabilities of the firms participating in their markets (although they may require collateral or margin to be posted for some activities, and they may monitor the financial condition of exchanges).[3] These and other general differences may exist because of the various missions and risks to financial stability that the agencies address.

A specific event in the financial industry is often regulated by multiple agencies because firms subject to institution-based regulation often conduct financial transactions that that are subject to activity-based regulation. JPMorgan's losses in derivatives markets in 2012 may provide a helpful illustration. JPMorgan's depository bank subsidiary had a risk management unit called CIO. This unit had significant losses on trades related to complex derivatives (called the London Whale trades at the time), which JPMorgan asserted were designed to guard against systemic risk. When revelations of the losses became public, and people wanted to know who JPMorgan's regulator was, the answer was that there were many regulators related to JPMorgan's London Whale trades, depending upon which aspect of the event a person was interested in.

The regulatory policy areas of agencies related to JPMorgan's derivatives trades are presented in *Figure 1*. As a bank, JPMorgan's risk management was subject to prudential regulation by the OCC at the depository level, and by the Federal Reserve on a consolidated basis at the holding company level. As a public company, JPMorgan's disclosures of the trades to its stockholders were regulated by the SEC. As a participant in derivatives markets, JPMorgan's transactions were subject to CFTC regulation. As an insured depository institution, JPMorgan's safety and soundness was also subject to the FDIC.

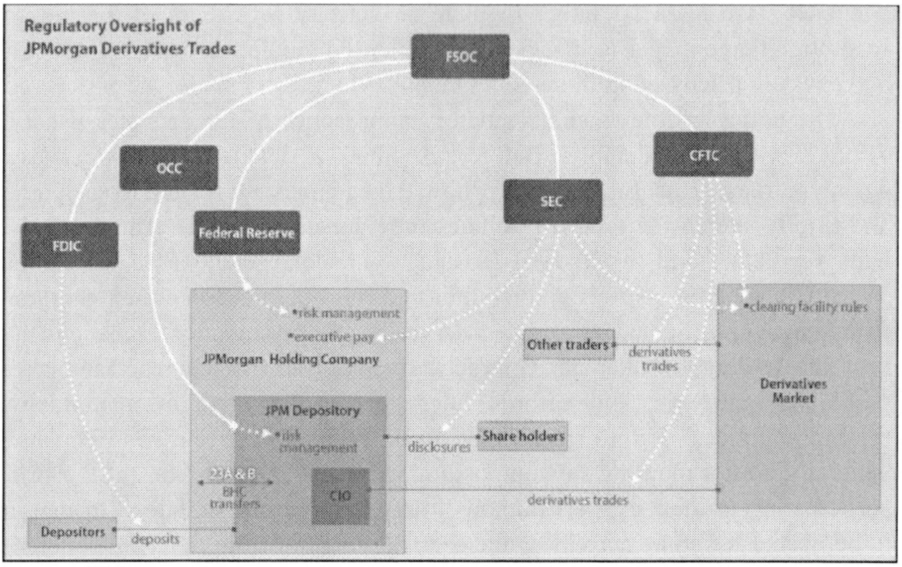

Source: CRS.

Figure 1. An Example of Regulation of JPMorgan Derivatives Trades.

Table 2 compares the general policy options and approaches of the banking regulators to the securities market regulators, which is drawn from *Banking Regulation versus Securities Regulation*, by Franklin Allen and Richard Herring. The table lists many of the categories of regulations that are often considered for banks and securities markets. It does not mean that each category is in place at all times; for example, there have been times during which the United States has restricted interest payments on bank deposits, and times when the United States has not. Many of these categories of policy options are discussed in more detail in later sections of this report.

In Allen's and Herring's view, banking regulatory policies and securities regulatory policies are directed at fundamentally different problems. They view bank regulation as being directed at *systemic risk*, which may be loosely defined as risk faced by the financial system as a whole, distinct from the costs and benefits faced by the failure or losses of a single firm or a price movement in a single market. In contrast, they attribute many of the securities market regulator's policies to *investor protection* and *efficiency enhancement* (including aligning corporate management with stockholder interests). Therefore, it may be useful to compare the general policy problems of banking and securities markets.

This report is organized as follows. The first section briefly discusses several policy problems associated with financial intermediation. The second section describes various modes of financial regulation to address these concerns and includes a table identifying the major federal regulators and the types of institutions and markets they supervise. The table also identifies certain emergency authorities available to the regulators, including those that relate to systemic financial disturbances. The third section focuses on the regulation of firms with bank charters. The fourth section focuses on the regulation of financial trading markets, especially securities and derivatives. The fifth section focuses on certain other financial regulators and markets that either do not easily fit into banking or securities or markets that do not have a dedicated regulator.

Table 2. Policies for Banking Regulation and Securities Regulation

Types of Banking Regulatory Policies	Types of Securities Regulatory Policies
Asset Restrictions	Disclosure Standards
Capital Adequacy	Registration Requirements
Conduct of Business Rules	Manipulation Prohibition
Competition Policy (Anti-Trust)	Insider Trading Prohibition
Conflict of Interest Rules	Takeover Rules
Investment Requirements	Protection of Minority Shareholders
Customer Suitability Rules	Investment Management Rules
Deposit Insurance	
Fit and Proper Entry Tests	
Limits on Interest on Deposits	
Limits on Interest on Loans	
Liquidity Requirements	
Reporting Large Transactions	
Reserve Requirements	
Restrictions on Geographic Reach	
Restrictions on Services and Product Lines	

Source: Banking Regulation versus Securities Regulation, Franklin Allen and Richard Herring, Wharton Financial Institutions Center, 2001.

The appendices topics include organizational differences among financial firms, the rating system that regulators use to evaluate the health of banks, the regulatory structure prior to the Dodd-Frank Act, a list of common acronyms, and a glossary of common financial terms.

Policy Problems in Banking and Securities Markets

Ultimately, the function of the financial system is to coordinate the flow of resources from savers to borrowers, and back again. Two common methods to provide this financial intermediation include (1) firms that directly gather funds from savers to directly lend to borrowers (banks, for example) and (2) markets that facilitate the trading of financial obligations (securities and derivatives exchanges, for example). The range of financial obligations includes, but is not limited to,

- debts—repayment of principal and interest,
- equities—share in ownership and returns,
- hybrids—mixture of debt and equity features,
- insurance—payment contingent on occurrence of a future event,
- swaps—promises to exchange one type of stream of payment for another, and
- forwards—promises for future delivery at a particular place and time.

Although there are many ways to organize a firm that offers bank-like services, and there are many types of contracts that combine elements of bank-like loans with securities contracts, the regulation of the financial system in the United States has historically focused on distinguishing banks, securities markets, and insurance.

The analytical tradition in the United States has been to distinguish commercial banking from investment banking. Commercial banks accept customer deposits and offer commercial loans. Investment banks underwrite and register new securities and market them to individual or institutional investors. Investment banks also provide brokerage services, advice on corporate financing and proprietary trading, and assistance to merger and acquisition proposals.

Although insurance issues are beyond the scope of this report, banking and securities markets are discussed briefly below.

Banks

Banks are intermediaries between savers and borrowers. In its simplest form, the business model of commercial banks is to accept deposits from savers in order to make loans to borrowers—in other words, banks borrow from depositors and offer loans to individuals, business firms, nonprofits, and governments. Although savers could offer loans directly to potential borrowers, there are several advantages of relying on specialized lenders. For example, savers essentially pay banks to act on their behalf (an agency relationship[4]), identifying credit-worthy borrowers, writing and administering loan contracts, and enforcing the loan terms if the borrower defaults. Another potential source of profit centers on timing. Since long-term interest rates are generally higher than short-term interest rates, banks can earn profits by borrowing short-term in order to offer longer-term loans (often referred to as a maturity transformation or maturity mismatch).

This is not an exhaustive list of commercial bank services or earnings, but it is a useful list to illustrate several recurring economic issues.

The business model of banks also creates a number of economic policy problems. Like any other agency relationship, bank managers do not necessarily always act in the best interests of bank investors or depositors. The maturity mismatch makes banks vulnerable to interest rate volatility and to "runs" if depositors withdraw their funds simultaneously in a panic. The effort to identify credit-worthy borrowers and projects can cause bankers to affect pools of borrowers in ways that create credit shortages, or base lending decisions on criteria that do not further social goals of the community (e.g., discrimination).

These policy problems may be addressed by regulations for individual banks. Some of these regulations include restrictions on conflicts of interest of bank managers, the use of deposits, and the ability of depositors to withdraw their funds; limitations on the proportion of bank resources that can be devoted to or drawn from particular markets or counterparties; rules on the loan application process; and laws to prevent lending discrimination.

Banking is also subject to systemic problems beyond the activities of any one institution. Another potential source of profit (related to the agency relationship) is for the bank to take excessive risk. That is, compared with other banks, an individual bank can keep fewer resources available against the possibility of depositor withdrawal, or offer more loans in the heightened-risk categories (that typically pay higher interest), and depend on its ability to borrow from other banks if it suffers excessive withdrawals or higher defaults. Although a single bank that follows a higher-risk strategy might be able to borrow from other banks if it suffers higher than expected losses or greater than expected depositor withdrawals, all banks cannot successfully follow this strategy simultaneously because there would be too few healthy banks to borrow from should loan defaults be higher than expected or should depositors withdraw funds in greater amounts than expected.

This systemic banking problem involves a fallacy of composition, and it can be illustrated using the example of a stadium. If a single person stands at the stadium, it is likely that the person will be able to see the event better, but if everyone stands in the stadium, most people will not have a better view of the event and will be less comfortable. Similarly, if a single bank expands its lending for a given amount of capital, that bank is likely to make higher profits without endangering financial stability, but if many banks follow a similar strategy, none gains a competitive advantage over the others, and all are less able to obtain interbank loans during a crisis.

Excessive risk taking by banks can have systemic consequences. One systemic problem may be that a large number of banks will attempt to borrow from each other at the same time, causing a spike in interest rates or the absence of new bank credit altogether. If many banks follow this strategy, then all banks may be unable to find an institution willing and able to lend to them in the event of depositor withdrawals, and the banking system as a whole may temporarily cease to be a source of credit for the wider economy.

Banks might contribute to a boom-bust cycle for debt-sensitive assets. During booms, banks that intend to rely on emergency lending from other banks may offer too much credit, and on terms that do not adequately account for the risk that the bank's own access to credit may decline if market conditions change. The resulting cheap credit may help fuel a price bubble in the asset or trading activity financed with the debt. During busts, more banks are likely to fail than would have occurred if banks had reserved the appropriate amount of resources for the amount of risk that they incurred. Thus, the higher bank failure rate (compared to if more banks had been cautious during the boom) could cause the total amount of credit available to the wider economy to shrink more than would have occurred if financial risks had been adequately accounted for.

There are a number of possible policy responses to these systemic concerns in banking. Bank regulators can be empowered to restrict bank balance sheets. Some of these restrictions, discussed in more detail below, include safety and soundness regulation and requirements to hold adequate capital. Even though these regulations may be applied at the institution level, they have systemic effects because in the aggregate the lending activity of the banking system as a whole has an important impact on credit booms and busts. Bank depositors could be offered insurance to reduce their incentive to withdraw funds. Banks that cannot borrow from other banks during emergencies can be provided a lender of last resort.

Markets to Trade Securities, Futures, and Other Contracts

In contrast to a commercial banking institution that originates and holds loans, a securities market is just a venue to exchange financial contracts. Markets can facilitate the trading of debts, equities, futures, or a variety of other financial instruments. Financial institutions that help facilitate the marketing of debts, equities and other financial instruments are sometimes called investment banks.

Although these financial markets are being presented as an alternative to commercial banking, there is no reason that a commercial bank would be unable to participate in securities markets as either a buyer or a seller (although in some cases it may be unlawful to do so). Loans to the government of the United States may be a useful illustration. While it is possible for a single bank to originate and hold an individual loan to the U.S. government, the borrowing of the government is overwhelmingly conducted by issuing debts (Treasury securities) that are traded. Banks are just one group among the many buyers of U.S. Treasury securities. Private firms have also issued tradable debt securities for centuries. Like lending institutions, tradable contracts have a long history and are subject to a number of well-known potential market failures.

Several enduring economic inefficiencies related to securities markets are caused by the limited availability of information and potential conflicts of interest. Some market participants may have an information advantage—such as providers of confidential services to financial firms. A related issue is the "lemons problem," named for the used-car market in which potential buyers of used cars might discount all used cars because of the fear that used-car salesmen may withhold negative information about the quality of a specific car being offered. Potential securities buyers may fall prey to securities dealers and brokers if the latter have an incentive to help place securities that the seller knows may have some undisclosed flaw (lemons). Furthermore, like any agent[5] relationship, securities professionals may not always act in the best interests of their clients.

Other potential economic inefficiencies can arise that are related to specific types of contracts that are traded. For example, some financial contracts are for future delivery of a physical commodity, such as wheat of a certain quality and quantity, at a particular place and time (forward or futures contract). This means that at any time, for example, there will be both a spot market for wheat (its price to be obtained currently) and the forward price (the current price for delivery on the specified future date). If there is no formal organization of trading rules, it might be possible for someone to use forward contracts to lock up most of the deliverable supply on a specific future date, leaving only a "corner" of the spot market for sale on that date. But even if such attempts to corner commodity markets are rarely successful, the attempts themselves might introduce additional price distortions that could contribute to financial instability.

Potential economic inefficiencies are also related to formal trading organizations and platforms, if they are used. Having experienced many of the policy problems described above, financial traders have from time to time organized formal market exchanges, adopted rules of trading, and limited membership. However, the exchange itself can then become a potential source of financial instability if it does not have enough resources to withstand the failure of one of its members to honor its obligations to the exchange, or if its rules exacerbate the problems described above. For example, nonmembers of the exchange could lose confidence (and willingness to participate) if they feel that members have important trading advantages, such as if the trades of members are executed first even if they are not submitted first.

There are a number of policy responses to concerns related to trading financial contracts. Some are listed in *Table 2*, including requiring that securities and traders be registered and investors be provided adequate disclosures regarding the characteristics of the securities. Given that formal exchanges are organized in part to address some of the known inefficiencies, policymakers might require that certain types of contracts be traded on formal exchanges. The organization and membership of the formal exchanges could be regulated. Providers of securities-related services may be regulated for minimum professional qualifications and potential conflicts of interest. Issuers of new securities may be required to meet certain financial thresholds and disclose specific information in a format and venue that is readily accessible to the investing public. Some potential buyers of securities may be excluded for lack of sufficient financial literacy or sophistication or have to exceed a minimum financial wherewithal (as a proxy or substitute for sophistication).

Securities markets may also create systemic concerns. Like bank lending, if securities markets fail to adequately address the risks of the activities being funded (thus overstating potential rewards compared with risks), then "too much" savings may be channeled into a particular asset class. As a result, prices in that asset class will tend to be bid up until the true risks manifest themselves, at which time the market collapses. Leveraged and collateralized funding can also cause securities markets to contribute to a boom-bust cycle. That is, if securities buyers are able to increase their purchasing power with debt, especially if the purchased securities form the collateral of the loan, then a decline in the price of the security can lead to "fire sales" as the loans taken out by the buyers default, and then the securities purchased with the loans are liquidated in an already falling market. Some are concerned that algorithmic or program trading can also contribute to systemic events if unanticipated events or technical shortcomings cause trading algorithms, which may be on autopilot, to pursue extreme strategies.

A number of possible policies can address systemic concerns in securities markets. One approach is to temporarily halt trading if market prices vary by more than some pre-specified amount during a set time. Another approach is to limit the amount, and collateral, of debt that can be used to fund securities purchases under some circumstances. Yet another approach is to require firms that facilitate securities issuance to retain some of the risk of the securities issued, sometimes referred to as *skin in the game*.

The Shadow Banking System

As discussed above, banking and securities markets are not mutually exclusive, nor are all financial obligations easily categorized. The term *shadow banking* is sometimes used to refer to the funding of loans through securities markets instead of banks—or to the funding of banks through securities markets instead of deposits. Other times, shadow banking is used to refer to financial activity that is ineligible for a government backstop. One type of government backstop is a financial guarantee, such as deposit insurance. Another type is access to emergency loans from the government, such as the ability to borrow from the Federal Reserve's discount window. What the definitions have in common is they describe alternatives to the simplistic banking model, that is, alternatives to banks that are funded with insured deposits and that only offer commercial loans.

Parts of the shadow banking system are regulated. For example, a lender could borrow money through securities markets rather than from traditional retail depositors. One way to do that is through a repurchase agreement (repo), in which the lender sells a security (such as a U.S. Treasury) today and promises to repurchase it in the near future at a higher price. The price differential represents a form of interest payment similar to a collateralized loan. Thus, rather than a bank borrowing money from traditional depositors, a bank can borrow from other financial institutions through repos. If a chartered bank signs a repo with a chartered bank, both firms are banks and both are regulated; nevertheless, under some definitions the transaction would be considered shadow banking. However, chartered banks are not the only firms that can use repurchase agreements—non-banks can raise funds through repurchase agreements in order to fund other investments, including loans. If a non-bank signs a repo with a non-bank, and uses the proceeds to fund other investments, neither non-bank may be subject to prudential regulation, have access to the Federal Reserve's discount window, have creditors with deposit insurance.

The repos described above are only one of many alternatives to deposits that can be used to fund loans. Other examples include relatively short-term commercial debt that is backed by pools of loans (asset-backed commercial paper, or ABCP). A bank could sponsor a facility that issues ABCP in order to buy loans. If so, the bank's participation (usually promising to provide liquidity if the market is unexpectedly disrupted) is subject to prudential regulation. As with repos, banks are not the only firms that can sponsor ABCP; thus, it is possible for the market to be funded by firms without access to the Fed's discount window and without insured deposits. However, activities being called shadow banking are often still subject to securities regulation.

Many of the general policy problems of banks and securities markets also apply to shadow banking. For example, if a class of loans (such as mortgages or sovereign debt) is funded through securities markets, potential flaws in securities issuance and pricing can contribute to a boom-bust cycle in assets purchased with those loans. If nonbanks (such as money market mutual funds and hedge funds) invest a fraction of the funds they gather, and promise to allow their own investors to withdraw funds at will, these nonbanks can suffer runs if many investors attempt to withdraw simultaneously. The reach of financial regulators to address policy problems in shadow banking varies from activity to activity and from class of firm to class of firm.

WHAT FINANCIAL REGULATORS DO

The regulatory missions of individual agencies vary, sometimes as a result of historical accident. Some agencies have powers over particular firms, but not over all of the other participants in the market that the firm might participate in. Other regulators have authority over markets or activities, and this authority applies to a variety of the firms that participate. As a result, a single firm might have to answer to both the regulator of its charter and to the regulator of a particular activity (i.e., regulatory overlap). However, there may also be instances in which a corner of the financial system has neither a regulator of the specific firms, nor a regulator of the particular activities (i.e., regulatory gap). This section of the report summarizes several categories of regulation, provides a table of specific financial regulators in the United States and their policy spheres, and describes the basic regulatory approach for banks (prudence) and securities markets (disclosure).

Regulatory Architecture and Categories of Regulation

The term *regulatory architecture* describes the organization of the agencies that regulate a particular policy sphere. A possible architecture is to have a single regulatory agency with examination powers over all industry firms, rulemaking authority for all industry-related activities, and power to enforce its rules and resolve controversies that arise in the industry. An alternative architecture is to have specialized regulators that focus on a subset of industry-related policy problems.

The United States has historically provided one or more regulator for each category of financial regulation, rather than a single agency with authority for all financial markets, activities, and institutions. From time to time, the perceived drawbacks to the multiplicity of federal regulators bring forth calls for regulatory consolidation. Even prior to the financial panic in September 2008, the Department of the Treasury had issued a framework for financial reform.[6] After the crisis, the legislative debate over the Dodd-Frank Act included different views on the topic: early versions of the Senate bill would have replaced all the existing bank regulators with a single Financial

Institution Regulatory Authority. Dodd-Frank created two new agencies (and numerous regulatory offices) and merged the Office of Thrift Supervision (OTS) with the Office of the Comptroller of the Currency (OCC).

Choosing a regulatory architecture may involve trade-offs. As one economist explained,

> On the one hand, one might conclude that the need to compete with other agencies would motivate a regulator to perform its tasks as effectively and efficiently as possible. On the other hand, one might argue that the desire to attract more clients could drive a regulatory agency to be loose.[7]

In addition, it is not clear that countries with single regulators fare better during crises or are more successful at preventing them. For example, the 2008 financial crisis damaged the financial systems of countries with significantly different regulatory approaches. While the U.S. response was to create a single council to coordinate its varied regulators, the United Kingdom (UK) in May 2010 broke up its Financial Services Authority, which had jurisdiction over securities, banking, derivatives, and insurance.

Here is a description of different ways to regulate financial firms and services:

- *Regulate Certain Types of Financial Institutions.* Some firms become subject to federal regulation when they obtain a particular business charter, and several federal agencies regulate only a single class of institution. Depository institutions are a good example: a depository may be subject to the regulations of multiple prudential regulators, but typically only one agency is granted primary oversight authority based on the bank's charter—national bank, state bank, credit union, etc.—and the choice of charter may not greatly affect the institution's permissible business mix. Government-sponsored enterprises (GSEs) also have a primary prudential regulator.

  Regulation keyed to particular institutions has at least two perceived disadvantages. First, regulator shopping, or *regulatory arbitrage*, may occur if regulated entities can choose their regulator. Second, unchartered firms engaging in the identical business activity as regulated firms may escape institutional regulation altogether.
- *Regulate a Particular Market.* Some markets become subject to federal financial regulation when they host the trading of covered

financial products. The New York Stock Exchange (NYSE) and the Chicago Mercantile Exchange (CME) are two examples. The Securities and Exchange Commission (SEC) regulates the trading of stocks and bonds and the Commodity Futures Trading Commission (CFTC) regulates the trading of commodity futures. The SEC and CFTC generally do not regulate the prices of stocks or futures traded on the exchanges; rather, they regulate the organization and membership of the exchanges, rules for trading, and attempt to prevent fraud, conflicts of interest, or manipulation by market participants.

Regulation keyed to markets has at least two perceived disadvantages. First, market evolution can create jurisdictional ambiguities among the regulators. Second, innovation in financial products may create regulatory gaps.

- *Regulate a Particular Financial Activity.* Some financial activities are subject to federal regulation no matter which institutions engage in them and no matter who hosts the trades in them. For example, the Consumer Financial Protection Bureau (CFPB) regulates certain classes of loans to consumers no matter who extends the loan (bank or nonbank). If the lender is a bank, the lender has to comply with both the regulations of the CFPB and the rules of its bank regulator.

  Regulation keyed to activities can be problematic. As discussed above, there are often multiple methods to achieve similar financial objectives (combining different contracts). Therefore, if one type of transaction is regulated, it may be possible for people to use another type of contract, one that is not currently regulated or through institutions that are not regulated.
- *Regulate for Systemic Risk.* One definition of systemic risk is that it occurs when each firm manages risk rationally from its own perspective, but the sum total of those decisions produces systemic instability under certain conditions. Similarly, regulators charged with overseeing individual parts of the financial system may satisfy themselves that no threats to stability exist in their respective sectors, but fail to detect risks arising from the interaction of firms and markets. Yet, regulation of institutions, markets, and activities may also have a component of systemic risk regulation. For example, regulation of bank capital may affect the potential for booms and busts in asset markets. The Dodd-Frank Act created the Financial Stability Oversight Council (FSOC) to assume a coordinating role

among the heads of financial regulatory agencies; the FSOC has a permanent staff to monitor financial-sector risks as a whole.

What does it mean to be regulated?

It is common to refer to a firm or a market as being regulated or unregulated. However, this simplification can mask important distinctions for any given policy discussion because regulators can have limited scope of operation. That is, agencies may have rulemaking authority or enforcement powers to address one set of policy concerns but not for other policy issues. Firms may be subject to different regulators for different aspects of their business.

The point can be illustrated with a more familiar industry. Are restaurants regulated? There is no federal Department of Restaurants; however, the Occupational Safety and Health Administration (OSHA) can make rules for worker safety (including food service employees), and the Department of Justice can enforce employment discrimination laws (including in restaurants). Furthermore, restaurants are typically subject to state and local health inspectors and related laws. If the policy topic is health and safety, it would be inaccurate to characterize restaurants as unregulated. On the other hand, many potential policy issues related to restaurants are typically unregulated. For example, the restaurant menu and prices are not typically regulated. A food service is typically free to pair nonstandard items (white wine with red meat) and charge very high prices.

Are financial institutions, markets, and activities regulated? Like the restaurant example above, the answer depends on the policy issue being discussed. Take the example of stocks. Firms with outstanding common stock must register with the SEC, file a prospectus, and make regular public disclosures. Marketplaces that facilitate stock market trading must register and comply with SEC regulations. However, the price of an individual stock is not typically regulated, and the amount of stock that an individual firm wishes to offer for sale is not typically regulated. However, even stock prices and trading volume may be subject to circuit breakers to temporarily limit trading during periods of exceptional volatility.

The information in *Table 3* sets out the general federal financial regulatory architecture for banks and securities markets. *Appendix D* contains a pre-Dodd-Frank version of the same table. Supplemental material—charts that illustrate the differences between banks, bank holding companies, and financial holding companies—appears in *Appendix B*.

Table 3. Federal Financial Regulators and Who They Supervise

Regulatory Agency	Institutions Regulated	Emergency/Systemic Risk Powers	Other Notable Authority
Federal Reserve	Bank holding companies and certain subsidiaries, financial holding companies, securities holding companies, savings and loan holding companies, and any firm designated as systemically significant by the FSOC. State banks that are members of the Federal Reserve System, U.S. branches of foreign banks, and foreign branches of U.S. banks. Payment, clearing, and settlement systems designated as systemically significant by the FSOC, unless regulated by SEC or CFTC.	Lender of last resort to member banks (through discount window lending) In "unusual and exigent circumstances," the Fed may extend credit beyond member banks, to provide liquidity to the financial system, but not to aid failing financial firms. May initiate resolution process to shut down firms that pose a grave threat to financial stability (requires concurrence of two-thirds of the FSOC). The FDIC and the Treasury Secretary have similar powers.	Numerous market-level regulatory authorities, such as checking services, lending markets, and other banking-related activities.
Office of the Comptroller of the Currency (OCC)	National banks, federally chartered thrift institutions		
Federal Deposit Insurance Corporation (FDIC)	Federally insured depository institutions, including state banks	After making a determination of systemic risk, the FDIC may invoke broad	Operates a deposit insurance fund for federally and state chartered banks and

Table 3. (Continued)

Regulatory Agency	Institutions Regulated	Emergency/Systemic Risk Powers	Other Notable Authority
	and thrifts that are not members of the Federal Reserve System.	authority to use the deposit insurance funds to provide an array of assistance to depository institutions, including debt guarantees.	thrifts.
National Credit Union Administration (NCUA)	Federally chartered or insured credit unions	Serves as a liquidity lender to credit unions experiencing liquidity shortfalls through the Central Liquidity Facility.	Operates a deposit insurance fund for credit unions, known as the National Credit Union Share Insurance Fund (NCUSIF).
Securities and Exchange Commission (SEC)	Securities exchanges, brokers, and dealers; clearing agencies; mutual funds; investment advisers (including hedge funds with assets over $150 million) Nationally recognized statistical rating organizations Security-based swap (SBS) dealers, major SBS participants, and SBS execution facilities Corporations selling securities to the public must register and make financial disclosures.	May unilaterally close markets or suspend trading strategies for limited periods.	Authorized to set financial accounting standards in which all publicly traded firms must use.
Commodity Futures Trading Commission (CFTC)	Futures exchanges, brokers, commodity pool operators, and commodity trading advisors Swap	May suspend trading, order liquidation of positions during market emergencies.	

Regulatory Agency	Institutions Regulated	Emergency/Systemic Risk Powers	Other Notable Authority
	dealers, major swap participants, and swap execution facilities		
Federal Housing Finance Agency (FHFA)	Fannie Mae, Freddie Mac, and the Federal Home Loan Banks	Acting as conservator (since Sept. 2008) for Fannie Mae and Freddie Mac	
Bureau of Consumer Financial Protection	Nonbank mortgage-related firms, private student lenders, payday lenders, and larger "consumer financial entities" to be determined by the Bureau Consumer businesses of banks with over $10 billion in assets Does not supervise insurers, SEC and CFTC registrants, auto dealers, sellers of nonfinancial goods, real estate brokers and agents, and banks with assets less than $10 billion		Writes rules to carry out the federal consumer financial protection laws

Source: The Congressional Research Service (CRS), with information drawn from agency websites, and financial regulatory legislation.

[a] See Appendix B.

REGULATING BANKS, THRIFTS, AND CREDIT UNIONS

In general, the term *bank* will be used in this section to refer to firms (or subsidiaries) with bank, thrift, or credit union charters.[8] Banking regulators in the United States attempt to address many of the general policy problems described in the introduction by focusing on the health of chartered banks. Bank charters limit the range of permissible activities and affiliations of banks. Bank regulators employ examiners to monitor and evaluate the financial health of the banks they regulate. Furthermore, deposit insurance and a system to coordinate bank reserves and provide emergency lending is available to participating banks. The primary prudential regulator of a given bank depends on its charter; however, other policies (such as lending to a troubled bank or resolving a failed bank) are applied by a single agency regardless of the charter. Activity-based regulation applies to chartered banks—thus the SEC retains its authority for communications between publicly traded banks and their stockholders, and the CFPB regulates many classes of loans that banks make to consumers.

Is this a bank?

Functionally, the simplest form of bank accepts deposits in order to offer loans.[9] Although this is not a legal definition of a bank, it does capture the basic intermediary function of banking. In practice, it is often difficult to precisely distinguish banking from other services.

It is tempting to ascribe this difficulty to financial innovation, but in reality many modern "innovations" are really just minor variations on old practices. Because in discussions of financial regulation, the term *bank* is often reserved for firms with specific charters, it may be useful to distinguish chartered-depository banks from other institutions and people who offer similar services.

Many institutions and organizations have offered bank-like services throughout history. For example, ancient Chinese records describe lenders that required borrowers to offer small goods as collateral for loans (similar to a modern pawn shop). People in Medieval Europe sometimes deposited precious metals with silversmiths (who had their own reasons for extra security) for safekeeping, and some silversmiths then offered loans to third parties, counting on the depositors to not withdraw simultaneously.

One controversial example is Whalebone Cafe Bank (WCB), an ice cream shop in Pittsburgh, Pennsylvania. Reportedly, customers can make a deposit at the ice cream shop and receive the equivalent of 5.5% interest in gift cards for ice cream and other goods sold at the store.[10] It has also been reported that WCB offered loans, including a $510-cash loan to a man who will pay it back in $60 installments, which includes a $25 fee. The Pennsylvania Department of Banking, according to reports, is investigating, but there are questions as to whether the agency can shut down an ice cream shop or ban stores from rewarding customers with gift cards.[11]

Several major banking laws limit their application to firms with federally insured deposits, specific banking charters, or affiliations with depository banks. As a result, some investment firms that are sometimes referred to as Wall Street banks are not banks for certain regulatory purposes, nor are some pawn shops and ice cream stores, even if they offer bank-like services.

As listed in *Table 1*, four prudential regulators coordinate the examinations policies of depositories through the Federal Financial Institution Examinations Council (FFIEC) in order to prevent inconsistencies in the stringency of regulatory oversight. A bank or thrift may organize itself with a depository subsidiary owned by a larger holding company, in which case the holding company may have a different primary regulator than the depository subsidiary. The OCC regulates depository banks and thrifts that have a federal charter (subsidiaries if in a holding company structure). The FDIC regulates banks with a state charter that are not members of the Federal Reserve System (subsidiaries if in a holding company structure). The NCUA regulates credit unions that have a federal charter. In addition to these federal regulators, state governments have their own agencies to administer state banking laws. The Federal Reserve regulates state-chartered member banks (subsidiaries) and holding companies of banks and thrifts. The Conference of State Bank Supervisors (CSBS) serves as a forum for state banking agencies, but is not itself a regulator. State banking supervisors choose a nonvoting representative to serve the FSOC in an advisory capacity.

Many prudential regulations are of degree, not of kind. That is, there are many categories of activities that banks may participate in, but they must either limit their concentration or offset related risks in another manner. For example, banks may offer 30-year fixed-rate mortgages; but, an individual bank may have to manage its resulting interest rate risk by offering other loans with shorter maturities or by acquiring derivatives that hedge interest rate risk. As a result, prudential regulation is not always about catching lawbreakers or policing legal violations, but is often about monitoring the risks that banks engage in or the procedures bank managers have in place to control risk. Even banks that have not violated any statute may be required to adjust their lending or other business practices in response to the regulator's evaluation of risks in current conditions.

This section describes five prominent elements of bank regulation that each primary prudential regulator supervises for its chartered firms: (1) safety and soundness, (2) capital requirements, (3) asset management, (4) consumer compliance, and (5) community reinvestment. In many cases the primary prudential regulator will not be the sole policymaker or regulatory authority for these issues. For example, rules for capital requirements and safety and soundness may be coordinated with other bank regulators, and banks may have to comply with consumer regulations issued by the CFPB in addition to satisfying their own primary prudential regulator. There may not be a clear delineation between each regulatory element; for example, adequate procedures for asset management might be important to maintain safety and soundness. *Appendix C* includes a discussion of the official ratings system that regulators apply to covered firms.

Safety and Soundness

Safety and soundness refers to a broad range of issues that relate to the health of a financial institution. Safety and soundness encompasses risk management, capital requirements, the diversification of a bank's portfolio, provisions for liquidity, allowances for loan and lease losses, concentrations of transactions with a single counterparty or in a single region, exposure to potentially expensive litigation, adequate training and expertise of management and staff, adequate procedures for internal controls, and many other issues. This section will not attempt to address all of the categories of safety and soundness regulation listed in *Table 2* above. Safety and soundness regulation is conducted prospectively—that is, banks can be examined prior to any indication of excess risk or any evidence of wrongdoing.

Safety and soundness regulation relates to economic policy issues because it can affect the credit cycle and conflicts of interest. The rapid decline in the price of one product (and thus a rapid rise in loan defaults by related firms, employees, etc.) is less likely to cause a wave of bank failures if banks are not permitted to concentrate their loan exposure to one industry or one line of business. Owners and counterparties of banks are more likely to effectively monitor bank managers if banks maintain clear and transparent systems of control.

Each loan has a variety of risk characteristics of concern to lenders and their regulators. Some of these risks can be estimated at the time the loan is issued. Credit risk, for example, is the risk that the borrower will fail to repay the principal of the loan as promised. Rising interest rates create another risk because the shorter-term interest rates that the lender often pays for its funds (e.g., deposit or CD rates) rise while the longer-term interest rates that the lender will receive from fixed-rate borrowers remain unchanged. Falling interest rates are not riskless either: fixed-rate borrowers may choose to repay loans early, reducing the lender's expected future cash flow. Federal financial regulators take into account expected default rates, prepayment rates, interest-rate exposure, and other risks when examining the loans issued by covered lenders.

The risk of a portfolio of bank assets is not just the sum of the risks of the individual loans and securities that make it up. Lenders can adjust the composition of their balance sheets to reduce or enhance the risks of the individual loans that make it up. A lender with many loans exposed to prepayment risk when interest rates fall, for example, could compensate by acquiring some assets that rise in value when interest rates fall. One example of a compensating asset would be an interest-rate derivative contract. Lenders are required to keep capital in reserve against the possibility of a drop in value of loan portfolios or other risky assets. Federal financial regulators take into account compensating assets, risk-based capital requirements, and other prudential standards when examining the balance sheets of covered lenders.

When regulators determine that a bank is taking excessive risks, or engaging in unsafe and unsound practices, they have a number of tools at their disposal to reduce risk to the institution (and ultimately to the federal deposit insurance fund). They can require banks to reduce specified lending or financing practices, dispose of certain assets, and order banks to take steps to restore sound balance sheets. In enforcement, regulators have "life-or-death" options, such as withdrawing deposit insurance, revoking the charter, or taking over a failing bank. In practice, bank regulators rarely use draconian tactics, and banks are given an opportunity to address concerns raised during an examination if the failure of the bank is not imminent.

Capital Requirements

As a general accounting concept, capital refers to the equity of a business—the amount by which its assets exceed its liabilities.[12] The more capital a firm has, the greater its capacity to absorb losses and remain solvent. Capital is related to leverage (various measures of the firm's reliance on debt and derivatives to fund its activities); firms that fund themselves with more equity capital (instead of debt) tend to have lower leverage ratios.

Capital regulation relates to economic policy problems because it can affect the credit cycle. One way higher bank capital affects the credit cycle is its potential to make the banking system more resilient during downturns. Unexpected loan losses are less likely to cause a bank to fail if it holds more capital. In the aggregate, higher capital requirements will tend to make the banking system more resilient because distressed banks may drain other banks of their liquid reserves while general liquidity is declining. On the other hand, banks are part of a broader financial system, therefore it may be possible that higher capital requirements for banks might not make the system as a whole safer if the cost of capital causes more financial activity to migrate to securities markets or shadow banking.

Capital regulation can also affect the credit cycle by affecting the amount of bank credit made available. Higher bank capital requirements tend to lower the leverage that banks can achieve, which reduces the potential lending that the banking system can offer to the broader economy. Whether higher capital requirements for banks lower total lending in the economy is more difficult to determine because it depends in part on how securities markets and shadow banking react.

Financial regulators require the institutions they supervise to maintain specified minimum levels of capital—defined in various ways—to increase the resilience of firms to shocks and to minimize losses to investors, customers, and taxpayers when failures occur. The riskiness of a bank's business model affects its capital requirements; for example, a bank that specializes in relatively risky credit card lending may have higher effective capital requirements than a bank that has a relatively safer and more diversified portfolio of commercial lending. Capital requirements, if they are set above what a firm would choose on its own, represent a cost to businesses because they reduce the amount of funds that may be loaned or invested in the market. Thus, there is a perpetual tension: individual banks adjust their own capital ratio to maximize profits, whereas regulators continually modify capital standards to either prevent excessive risk-taking or to promote the availability of credit to the wider economy.

The actual capital held by banks should not be confused with statutory minimums. Banks may choose to hold excess capital if bank management believes that economic conditions may deteriorate. For example, in 2007 and 2008, JPMorgan executives referred to their portfolio as a "fortress balance sheet" in part because it was believed to be prepared for a worsening economic environment. Bank regulators may encourage regulated banks to hold additional capital to make the banking system more resilient. Following the financial turmoil of September 2008, banking regulators oversaw an increase in bank capital without the need for new legislation, new notice and comment rulemaking, or new international negotiations because bank regulators can require changes by insured depositories under existing authority (whether due to encouragement of regulators or changed preferences for prudence by bank managers).

U.S. banking regulators cooperate with banking regulators in other countries. The general approach to capital standards are based on the Basel Accords, an international framework developed under the auspices of the Bank for International Settlements.[13] Although the Basel Accords use the term *requirement*, Basel capital standards are not enforceable if a member country does not implement them (unlike the WTO dispute resolution process, for example). In other words, each participating country sets its own capital standards, but member countries use the Basel framework to establish best practices and harmonize banking regulation. The Basel committee describes its function thusly:

> The Basel Committee on Banking Supervision provides a forum for regular cooperation on banking supervisory matters. Its objective is to enhance understanding of key supervisory issues and improve the quality of banking supervision worldwide. It seeks to do so by exchanging information on national supervisory issues, approaches and techniques, with a view to promoting common understanding. At times, the Committee uses this common understanding to develop guidelines and supervisory standards in areas where they are considered desirable. In this regard, the Committee is best known for its international standards on capital adequacy; the Core Principles for Effective Banking Supervision; and the Concordat on cross-border banking supervision.[14]

A guiding principle of the Basel standards is that capital requirements should be risk-based. The riskier an asset, the more capital a bank should hold against possible losses. Risk-based regulations can be more prudent than simple leverage ratios because two firms with identical amounts of debt may have very different probabilities of failure if their assets are different. For example, one might lend primarily to households (credit cards, mortgages, student loans, and auto loans), whereas the other lends primarily to manufacturing businesses or agricultural service providers.

One possible drawback of a risk-based capital adequacy approach is that the regulation may become procyclical. That is, the capital standards themselves may reinforce the tendency for the banking system to expand credit during economic booms and contract credit during economic busts as views of risk evolve. If so, then risk-based capital requirements will make it more difficult for macro-prudential regulators to mitigate asset bubbles when they form, and will make it more difficult to promote additional credit expansion during economic downturns.

Procyclicality could occur if economic forecasters and financial analysts are overconfident that stable economic environments will continue or are over-pessimistic during unstable economic environments. To the extent that evaluating the risk of a long-term asset involves evaluating the probability of future economic instability, over-confidence will lead to lower than optimal capital requirements and over-pessimism will lead to higher than optimal capital requirements. If regulators and market participants are using the same financial models with similar historical data, it is unlikely that the regulators would provide much of a check on some sources of procyclicality in a risk-based system because the regulators and the banks could have similar measures of risk. On the other hand, regulators could require additional stress tests for the system as a whole, which an individual firm would not have the incentive or ability to conduct.

Asset Management

Asset management refers to providing financial products or services to a third party for a fee or commission. Examples of asset management include personal fiduciary services, such as wealth management for private clients. Other examples include acting as a custodian, providing security holder services, and offering investment advice.

Regulation of asset management activities relates to economic policy issues because the asset management services of banks can have broader effects. An example of the relation of asset management to the policy issues is the custodian role of banks for some complex financial transactions. For example, some forms of interbank lending include collateral, but who will hold the collateral for the duration of the contract? If custodian banks mismanage the assets, then disruptions in interbank lending markets can be magnified during periods of financial turmoil. During financial instability, banks may be turning to collateralized lending precisely because they have greater desire for safety, certainty, and speed. Disruptions to asset management services, through either the failure of central custodian banks or slow processing of existing custodian banks, may reinforce other banks' fears of uncertainty and slow processing.

Banks are not the only firms that offer asset management services. Thus, as discussed above, bank regulators do not make rules for the entire asset management industry; rather, they issue guidance to the firms with particular charters, and they provide examinations to insure that chartered banks have procedures in place that are consistent with sound asset management principles.

Consumer Protection Compliance

Lenders must comply with a variety of statutes and regulations when offering financial products to consumers. Prior to the financial crisis, authority to oversee consumer financial protection had been spread among a number of banking regulators, HUD, and the FTC. The Dodd-Frank Act gathered much of this authority and personnel into a new Consumer Financial Protection Bureau (CFPB), but bank regulators still supervise many consumer activities of their chartered firms. One reason is that poor customer relations can be a threat to the safety and soundness of the institution, in part because it is usually bad for business. The banking agencies examine banks for compliance with consumer laws and assist in resolving consumer complaints.

Bank regulators can facilitate consumer compliance by offering an ombudsman to assist in resolving complaints. Ombudsman offices are usually separate from those of the safety and soundness examiners. Such offices may help insure that consumers receive a fair and expeditious resolution of their concerns with a firm that is regulated by that agency. This may help reduce the time and expense of more formal complaint resolution options where consumers might otherwise seek redress (such as courts).

Some rulemaking activity for consumer compliance is shared between the CFPB and the bank regulators. For example, the CFPB has issued rules for appraisals of residential properties and mortgages. However, banks also rely on appraisals to establish collateral for their mortgage loans; thus, both the CFPB and bank regulators are involved in rulemaking for residential real estate appraisals.

Regulators of Firms with Bank Charters

In many cases, depository banks are owned within a larger holding company structure, and the primary prudential regulator of the holding company may not be the same as the primary prudential regulator of the bank subsidiary. There is a dual banking system, in which each depository institution is subject to regulation by its chartering authority: state or federal. In addition, because virtually all depository institutions are covered by federal deposit insurance, they are subject to at least one federal primary regulator (i.e., the federal authority responsible for examining the institution for safety and soundness and ensuring its compliance with federal banking laws).

The federal banking agencies are briefly discussed below, along with certain powers that these agencies have that are not limited to the firms of which each is the primary prudential regulator.

Office of the Comptroller of the Currency

The Office of the Comptroller (OCC) was created in 1863 as part of the Department of the Treasury to supervise federally chartered banks (i.e., "national" banks) and to replace the circulation of state-bank notes with a single national currency (Chapter 106, 13 Stat. 99). The OCC is the primary prudential regulator for federally chartered banks and thrifts. The head of the OCC, the Comptroller of the Currency, is also a member of the board of the FDIC and a voting member of FSOC. Like the other prudential regulators described below, the OCC has examination powers to enforce its responsibilities for the safety and soundness of nationally chartered banks, and strong enforcement powers, including the ability to issue cease and desist orders and revoke the charter of covered firms.

In addition to institution-level examinations, the OCC oversees systemic risk among nationally chartered banks and thrifts. One example of OCC systemic surveillance is the regular survey of credit underwriting practices. This survey compares underwriting standards over time and assesses whether OCC examiners believe the credit risk of nationally chartered bank portfolios is rising or falling. In addition, the OCC publishes regular reports on the derivatives activities of U.S. commercial banks.

Federal Deposit Insurance Corporation

The FDIC was created in 1933 to provide assurance to small depositors that they would not lose their savings if their bank failed (P.L. 74-305, 49 Stat. 684). The FDIC is the primary federal prudential regulator of state-chartered banks that are not members of the Federal Reserve System. It has, to some extent, similar examination and enforcement powers for the firms it regulates, as the OCC has for federally chartered banks. In addition to its role as a prudential bank regulator, the FDIC administers a deposit insurance fund and resolves failing depositories and certain systemic non-banks.

Deposit insurance relates to economic policy issues because it may help to stabilize an important source of bank funding during times of financial turmoil. Prior to the 1930s, American financial crises were often accompanied by rapid withdrawal of deposits from banks rumored to be in trouble (or actually in trouble). Even prudent, well-managed banks could have difficulty surviving these runs by depositors. Federal deposit insurance assures depositors that the full-faith and credit of the federal government guarantees their deposits up to a preset level. Despite occasional periods of bank failures, banks with insured deposits have suffered almost no depositor runs since the establishment of deposit insurance. Banks are assessed premiums by the FDIC for the deposit coverage.

The agency provides deposit insurance to all federally insured banks and thrifts (but not credit unions). In 2008, as the financial crisis worsened, Congress passed a temporary increase in the deposit insurance ceiling from $100,000 to $250,000 for most accounts.[15] The increase was made permanent by the Dodd-Frank Act.

The deposit insurance system has been revised a number of times. For example, legislative reform (P.L. 109-173, 119 Stat. 3601) in the mid-2000s raised the coverage limit for retirement accounts to $250,000 and indexed both its limit and the general deposit insurance coverage ceiling to inflation. The reform act made changes to the risk-based assessment system to determine the payments of individual institutions. Within a range set by the reform act, the FDIC uses notice and comment rulemaking to set the designated reserve ratio (DRR) that supports the Deposit Insurance Fund (DIF). The FDIC uses its power to examine individual institutions and issue regulations for all insured-depository institutions to monitor and enforce safety and soundness.[16]

Using emergency authority it received under the Federal Deposit Insurance Corporation Improvement Act of 1991 (FDICIA; P.L. 102-242),[17] the FDIC made a determination of systemic risk in October 2008 and announced that it would temporarily guarantee (1) newly issued senior unsecured debt of banks, thrifts, and certain holding companies and (2) non-interest bearing deposit transaction accounts (e.g., business checking accounts), regardless of dollar amount.[18] Under Dodd-Frank, the FDIC's authority to guarantee bank debt is made explicit. Although the 2008 emergency measures have expired, the FDIC has the authority to create some programs during a possible future crisis.

The financial crisis of 2008 revealed a number of lessons related to bank runs and deposit insurance. Several non-banks suffered the equivalent of depositor runs, including money market mutual funds and the interbank repo market. Because the equivalent of depositor runs can occur in other financial activities, Dodd-Frank expanded the assessment base for FDIC premiums to include a bank's entire balance sheet, not just its insured deposits. Furthermore, creditors of failing financial institutions may, under extreme circumstances, be provided with additional guarantees if the failure is determined to be a threat to the financial stability of the United States.

When banks fail, the FDIC disposes the assets and liabilities. The FDIC manages the DIF, which is derived from risk-based assessments levied on depository institutions. The fund is used for various purposes, primarily for resolving failed or failing institutions. The FDIC has broad jurisdiction because nearly all banks and thrifts, whether federally or state-chartered, carry FDIC insurance.

The Dodd-Frank Act also expanded the FDIC's role in liquidating troubled financial institutions. Under the act, the Financial Stability Oversight Council (FSOC) will designate certain financial institutions—banks and nonbanks—as systemically important. In addition to more stringent capital regulation, those firms are required to draw up "living wills," or plans for orderly liquidation. The Federal Reserve, with the concurrence of two-thirds of the FSOC, may determine that a firm represents a "severe threat" to financial stability and may order it closed. The FDIC will administer the resolution process for nonbanks as well as banks.[19]

The Federal Reserve

The Federal Reserve System was established in 1913 to provide stability to banks and trusts through the regulation of reserves (P.L. 63-43, 38 STAT. 251). The Federal Reserve System has three components: the Federal Reserve Board (FRB), the regional Federal Reserve Banks (FRBNY, FRBSF, etc.), and the Open Market Committee. The Fed is the primary prudential regulator for a variety of lending institutions, including bank holding companies, certain U.S. branches of foreign banks, and state-chartered banks that are members of the Federal Reserve System. Under the Gramm-Leach-Bliley Act (GLBA; P.L. 106-102), the Fed serves as the umbrella regulator for financial holding companies, which are defined as conglomerates that are permitted to engage in a broad array of financially related activities. As a primary prudential regulator, the Federal Reserve has similar authority as the OCC.

In addition to the charter class that the Federal Reserve regulates, the Dodd-Frank Act made the Fed the primary regulator of all financial firms (bank or nonbank) that are designated as systemically significant by the FSOC (of which the Fed is a member). Capital requirements for such firms may be stricter than for other firms. In addition, Dodd-Frank made the Fed the principal regulator for systemically important financial-market utilities. The Fed also regulates savings and loan holding companies and securities holding companies, formerly defined in securities law as an investment bank holding company.

In addition to its powers as a primary prudential regulator, the Federal Reserve conducts monetary policy, monitors the financial system, acts as the fiscal agent of the United States, and regulates the payment system and a number of financial activities. Examples of additional activities regulated by the Fed (sometimes only as a monitor and sometimes jointly with other agencies) include equal credit opportunity (Reg-B), Community Reinvestment Act (CRA) related agreements (Reg-G), and extensions of credit by brokers and dealers (Reg-T). The list of regulatory topics now extends from Reg-A to Reg-YY.

National Credit Union Administration

The National Credit Union Administration (NCUA), originally part of the Farm Credit Administration, became an independent agency in 1970 (P.L. 91-206, 84 STAT. 49). The NCUA regulates all federal credit unions and those state credit unions that elect to be federally insured. It administers a Central Liquidity Facility, which is the credit union lender of last resort, and the National Credit Union Share Insurance Fund, which insures credit union deposits. Credit unions are member-owned financial cooperatives and must be not-for-profit institutions. As cooperatives, they are exempt from corporate income tax. Many credit unions offer similar services as community banks, and this differential tax treatment is often the subject of legislative proposals in each congressional session.

Regulating Securities, Derivatives, and Other Contract Markets

Regulators of financial trading attempt to address many economic policy problems. As discussed in the introductory sections, financial markets may not be level playing fields—some people with access to confidential information may have a trading advantage. Furthermore, the people who issue and market new securities (or derivatives) may have the incentive to withhold or mischaracterize some of the information they have about the securities or derivatives being offered. Even if these market facilitators provide full information, the outcome might still be less than optimal if other market participants simply believe that material information is not being disclosed or that insiders are behaving strategically. As a result, much of the regulation of securities and derivatives markets has focused on resolving conflicts of interest and requiring full disclosure of material information, unlike bank regulation that tends to focus on prudence. In addition, much securities market regulation has been applied through enforcement against afterthe-fact violations, rather than as prospective examinations of covered firms.

Non-Bank Financial Regulators

Securities and Exchange Commission

The SEC was created as an independent agency in 1934 to enforce newly written federal securities laws (P.L. 73-291, 48 Stat. 881). Although the SEC is concerned with ensuring the safety and soundness of the firms it regulates, its primary concern is maintaining fair and orderly markets and protecting investors from fraud. The SEC generally[20] does not have the authority to limit risks taken by non-bank financial institutions or the ability to prop up a failing firm, with some exceptions. Two types of firms come under the SEC's jurisdiction: (1) all corporations that sell securities to the public and (2) securities broker/dealers and other securities markets intermediaries.

Firms that sell securities—stocks and bonds—to the public are required to register with the SEC. Registration entails the publication of detailed information about the firm, its management, the intended uses for the funds raised through the sale of securities, and the risks to investors. The initial registration disclosures must be kept current through the filing of periodic financial statements: annual and quarterly reports (as well as special reports when there is a material change in the firm's financial condition or prospects).

Beyond these disclosure requirements, and certain other rules that apply to corporate governance, the SEC does not have any direct regulatory control over publicly traded firms. Bank regulators are expected to identify unsafe and unsound banking practices in the institutions they supervise and have the power to intervene and prevent banks from taking excessive risks. The SEC has no comparable authority; the securities laws simply require that risks be disclosed to investors. Registration with the SEC, in other words, is in no sense a government endorsement that a security is a good or safe investment.

To enable investors to make informed investment choices, the SEC has statutory authority over financial accounting standards. All publicly traded firms are required to use generally accepted accounting principles (GAAP), which are formulated by the Financial Accounting Standards Board (FASB), the American Institute of Certified Public Accountants (AICPA), and the SEC itself.

Besides publicly traded corporations, a number of securities market participants are also required to register with the SEC (or with one of the industry self-regulatory organizations that the SEC oversees). These include stock exchanges, securities brokerages (and numerous classes of their personnel), mutual funds, auditors, investment advisers, and others. To maintain their registered status, all these entities must comply with rules meant to protect investors' interests, prevent fraud, and promote fair and orderly markets. The area of SEC supervision most analogous to banking regulation is broker/dealer regulation. Several provisions of law and regulation protect brokerage customers from losses arising from brokerage firm failure. The Securities Investor Protection Corporation (SIPC), created by Congress in 1970, operates an insurance scheme funded by assessments on broker/dealers (and with a backup line of credit with the U.S. Treasury). SIPC guarantees customer accounts up to $500,000 for losses arising from brokerage failure or fraud (but not market losses). Unlike the FDIC, however, SIPC does not examine broker/dealers and has no regulatory powers.

Since 1975, the SEC has enforced a net capital rule applicable to all registered broker/dealers. The rule requires broker/dealers to maintain an excess of capital above mere solvency, to ensure that a failing firm stops trading while it still has assets to meet customer claims. Net capital levels are calculated in a manner similar to the risk-based capital requirements under the Basel Accords, but the SEC has its own set of risk weightings, which it calls "haircuts." The riskier the asset, the greater the haircut.

Although the net capital rule appears to be similar in its effects to the banking agencies' risk-based capital requirements, there are significant differences. The SEC has no authority to intervene in a broker/dealer's business if it takes excessive risks that might cause net capital to drop below the required level. Rather, the net capital rule is often described as a liquidation rule—not meant to prevent failures but to minimize the impact on customers. Moreover, the SEC has no authority comparable to the banking regulators' prompt corrective action powers: it cannot preemptively seize a troubled broker/dealer or compel it to merge with a sound firm.

The differences between bank and securities regulation with respect to safety and soundness came into sharp focus with the collapse of Bear Stearns, one of the five largest investment banks, in March 2008.[21] The SEC monitored Bear Stearns' financial condition until shortly before the collapse (which was precipitated by the refusal of other market participants to extend short-term credit to Bear Stearns), and it believed that the firm had sufficient levels of capital and liquidity. When bankruptcy suddenly loomed, it was the Federal Reserve that stepped in to broker the sale of Bear Stearns to JP Morgan Chase by agreeing to purchase $30 billion of "toxic" Bear Stearns assets.

The Bear Stearns situation highlighted several apparent anomalies in the U.S. regulatory structure. The SEC lacked safety and soundness powers over the institutions it supervised, and the Fed was forced to commit funds to an investment bank over which it had no regulatory jurisdiction. The anomaly became even more pronounced when the Fed subsequently established a lending facility to provide short-term credit to other investment banks.[22]

The Bear Stearns collapse showed the inability of the SEC to respond to a brokerage failure with systemic risk implications. There is more to the story, however, than the differences between bank regulation and the SEC's net capital rule. In 2004, the SEC devised a voluntary supervisory scheme for the largest investment banks, called the Consolidated Supervised Entities (CSE) program.[23] The CSE firms were all registered broker/dealers, but were also large holding companies with extensive operations carried on outside the broker/dealer unit. Thus, the SEC had no capital requirement that applied to the entire investment bank. Under CSE, this was to change: as a substitute for the net capital rule, the firms agreed to abide by the Basel risk-based standard and maintain that level of capital *at the holding company level.* On a voluntary basis, the firms agreed to grant the SEC the authority to examine and monitor their compliance, above and beyond the SEC's explicit statutory authority.[24]

Whatever the intent of the CSE program, it did not succeed in preventing excessive risk-taking by the participants.[25] By the end of September 2008, all five CSE investment banks had either failed (Lehman Brothers), merged to prevent failure (Merrill Lynch and Bear Stearns), or applied for bank holding company status (Morgan Stanley and Goldman Sachs).[26] On September 26, 2008, SEC Chairman Cox announced the end of the CSE program, declaring that "[t]he last six months have made it abundantly clear that voluntary regulation does not work. When Congress passed the Gramm-Leach-Bliley

Act, it created a significant regulatory gap by failing to give to the SEC or any agency the authority to regulate large investment bank holding companies."[27]

With the Dodd-Frank Act, Congress eliminated the investment bank holding company framework in Section 17 of the Securities Exchange Act of 1934. Section 618 of Dodd-Frank permits a securities holding company to be subject to consolidated supervision and submit to Federal Reserve regulation. Under Title I of Dodd-Frank, any securities firm that is deemed by the FSOC to be systemically significant will automatically come under the consolidated supervision of the Federal Reserve.

Other provisions of Dodd-Frank, however, gave the SEC new responsibilities that have aspects of safety and soundness regulation. Under Section 731, the SEC sets capital requirements for major security-based swap participants and security-based swap dealers. Section 956 gives the SEC new authority to prohibit compensation structures in broker/dealers and investment advisory firms that create inappropriate risks.

Commodity Futures Trading Commission

The CFTC was created in 1974 to regulate commodities futures and options markets, which at the time were poised to expand beyond their traditional base in agricultural commodities to encompass contracts based on financial variables, such as interest rates and stock indexes. The CFTC's mission is to prevent excessive speculation, manipulation of commodity prices, and fraud. Like the SEC, the CFTC oversees industry self-regulatory organizations (SROs)—the futures exchanges and the National Futures Association—and requires the registration of a range of industry firms and personnel, including futures commission merchants (brokers), floor traders, commodity pool operators, and commodity trading advisers.

The Dodd-Frank Act greatly expanded the CFTC's jurisdiction by eliminating exemptions for certain over-the-counter derivatives. As a result, swap dealers, major swap participants, swap clearing organizations, swap execution facilities, and swap data repositories are required to register with the CFTC. These entities are subject to business conduct standards contained in statute or promulgated as CFTC rules.

Like the SEC, the CFTC does not directly regulate the safety and soundness of individual firms, with the exception of newly regulated swap dealers and major swap participants, for whom it sets capital standards pursuant to Dodd-Frank.

Federal Housing Finance Agency

The FHFA was created in 2008 by the Housing and Economic Recovery Act of 2008 (P.L. 110- 289) to consolidate and strengthen regulation of a group of housing finance-related government-sponsored enterprises (GSEs): Fannie Mae, Freddie Mac, and the Federal Home Loan Banks.[28] The FHFA succeeded the Office of Federal Housing Enterprise Oversight (OFHEO) and the Federal Housing Finance Board (FHFB). FHFA authority includes both the safety and soundness authority of the former OFHEO and the housing mission goals for the GSEs that had been administered by HUD.

The impetus to create the FHFA came from concerns about risk— including systemic risk— arising from the rapid growth of the GSEs, particularly Fannie and Freddie. These two GSEs were profit-seeking, shareholder-owned corporations that took advantage of their government-sponsored status to accumulate undiversified investment portfolios of more than $1.5 trillion, consisting almost exclusively of home mortgages (and securities and derivatives based on those mortgages).

The FHFA was given enhanced safety and soundness powers resembling those of the federal bank regulators. These powers included the ability to set capital standards, order the enterprises to cease any activity or divest any asset that posed a threat to financial soundness, and replace management and assume control of the firms that became seriously undercapitalized.

One of the FHFA's first actions was to place both Fannie and Freddie in "voluntary" conservatorship.[29] Fannie and Freddie continue to operate, under an agreement with the U.S. Treasury. The Treasury provided capital to the two firms, by means of preferred stock purchases, to ensure that each remains solvent. In return, the government received warrants equivalent to a 79.9% equity ownership position in the firms.

Consumer Financial Protection Bureau

Title X of Dodd-Frank created the Consumer Financial Protection Bureau (CFPB) to bring the consumer protection regulation of depository and non-depository financial institutions into closer alignment.[30] The bureau is an independent entity within the Federal Reserve with authority over an array of consumer financial products and services (including deposit taking, mortgages, credit cards and other extensions of credit, loan servicing, check guaranteeing, collection of consumer report data, debt collection, real estate settlement, money transmitting, and financial data processing). CFPB serves as the primary federal consumer financial protection supervisor and enforcer of federal consumer protection laws over many of the institutions that offer these products and services.

However, the bureau's regulatory authority varies based on institution size and type. Regulatory authority differs for (1) depository institutions with more than $10 billion in assets, (2) depository institutions with $10 billion or less in assets, and (3) non-depositories. The Dodd-Frank Act also explicitly exempts a number of different entities and consumer financial activities from the bureau's supervisory and enforcement authority. Among the exempt entities are

- merchants, retailers, or sellers of nonfinancial goods or services, to the extent that they extend credit directly to consumers exclusively for the purpose of enabling consumers to purchase such nonfinancial goods or services;
- automobile dealers;
- real estate brokers and agents;
- financial intermediaries registered with the SEC or CFTC;
- insurance companies; and
- depository institutions with $10 billion or less in assets.

Regulatory Umbrella Groups

The need for coordination and data sharing among regulators has led to the formation of innumerable interagency task forces to study particular market episodes and make recommendations to Congress. Three interagency organizations have permanent status.

Financial Stability Oversight Council

Title I of the Dodd-Frank Act created the FSOC on the date of enactment.[31] The council is chaired by the Secretary of the Treasury, and the other voting members consist of the heads of the Federal Reserve, FDIC, OCC, NCUA, SEC, CFTC, FHFA, CFPB, and a member with insurance expertise appointed by the President.

Nonvoting members, serving in an advisory capacity, include the director of the Office of Financial Research (created by Title I to support the FSOC), the head of the Federal Insurance Office (created by Title V of Dodd-Frank), a state banking supervisor, a state insurance commissioner, and a state securities commissioner.

The FSOC is tasked with identifying risks to financial stability and responding to emerging systemic risks, while minimizing moral hazard arising from expectations that firms or their counterparties will be rescued from failure. The FSOC's duties include

- collecting information on financial firms from regulators and through the Office of Financial Research;
- monitoring the financial system to identify potential systemic risks;
- proposing regulatory changes to Congress to promote stability, competitiveness, and efficiency;
- facilitating information sharing and coordination among financial regulators;
- making regulatory recommendations to financial regulators, including "new or heightened standards and safeguards";
- identifying gaps in regulation that could pose systemic risk;
- reviewing and commenting on new or existing accounting standards issued by any standard-setting body; and
- providing a forum for the resolution of jurisdictional disputes among council members. The FSOC may not impose any resolution on disagreeing members, however.

The council is required to provide an annual report and testimony to Congress.

In contrast to some proposals to create a systemic risk regulator, the Dodd-Frank Act does not give the council authority (beyond the existing authority of its individual members) to eliminate emerging threats or close regulatory gaps it identifies. In most cases, the council can only make regulatory recommendations—it cannot impose change.

Although the FSOC does not have direct supervisory authority over any financial institution, it plays an important role in regulation, because firms that it designates as systemically important come under a consolidated supervisory regime that may be considerably more stringent than the standards that apply to non-systemic firms. The FSOC is also required to approve (by a two-thirds vote) decisions by the Federal Reserve to shut down systemically significant financial firms that pose a severe threat to financial stability.

Federal Financial Institution Examinations Council

The Federal Financial Institutions Examination Council (FFIEC) was created by legislation[32] in 1979 as a formal interagency body to coordinate federal regulation of lending institutions. Through the FFIEC, the federal banking regulators issue a single set of reporting forms for covered institutions. The FFIEC also attempts to harmonize auditing principles and supervisory decisions. The FFIEC is made up of the Federal Reserve, OCC, FDIC, NCUA, and CFPB. Except for the CFPB, the member agencies of the FFIEC are primary prudential regulators of depository institutions with specific charters as described above and employ examiners to enforce safety and soundness regulations for lending institutions. The examination powers of the CFPB for compliance with consumer protection rules varies across institutions, many of which may not have bank charters.

Federal financial institution examiners evaluate the risks of covered institutions. The specific safety and soundness concerns common to the FFIEC agencies can be found in the examiner's handbook to monitor lenders. Each subject area of the handbook can be updated separately. Examples of safety and soundness subject areas include important indicators of risk, such as capital adequacy, asset quality, liquidity, and sensitivity to market risk.

President's Working Group on Financial Markets

The President's Working Group on Financial Markets (PWG) was created by President Reagan through executive order in 1988.[33] The PWG includes the Secretary of the Treasury and the Chairmen of the Federal Reserve, the SEC, and the CFTC. It is not a formal agency subject to congressional oversight, although each member is subject to Senate confirmation at the time of appointment.

The impetus for the creation of the PWG was the stock market crash of October 1987, and specifically the role that the stock index futures markets (under CFTC jurisdiction) played in creating panic in the stock market (regulated by SEC). Studies conducted by the SEC, the CFTC, a blue-ribbon panel appointed by the President (the Presidential Task Force on Market Mechanisms, or Brady Commission), and the stock and futures exchanges reached strikingly different conclusions; the task of the PWG was to review the studies and issue a further report.

The PWG provides interagency coordination and information sharing and studies entities and products that raise intermarket regulatory issues, such as hedge funds and OTC derivatives. For example, in March 2008, the PWG issued a policy statement on the ongoing financial crisis.[34] Another example is the October 2010 PWG report called for changes to address systemic risk and reduce the susceptibility of money market mutual funds (MMFs) to runs.[35]

Non-Bank Capital Requirements

Federal Housing Finance Agency

The Federal Housing Finance Agency (FHFA) is authorized to set capital classification standards for the Federal Home Loan Banks, Fannie Mae, and Freddie Mac that reflect the differences in operations between the banks and the latter two GSEs.[36] The law defines several capital classifications and prescribes regulatory actions to be taken as a GSE's condition worsens. Limitations are placed on a GSE if it does not meet certain capital standards.

No growth in total assets is permitted for an *undercapitalized* GSE, unless (1) FHFA has accepted the GSE's capital restoration plan, (2) an increase in assets is consistent with the plan, and (3) the ratios of both total capital to assets and tangible equity to assets are increasing. An undercapitalized entity is subject to heightened scrutiny and supervision.

If a regulated entity is *significantly undercapitalized*, FHFA must take one or more of the following actions: elect new directors, dismiss directors or executives, and hire qualified executive officers, or other actions. Without prior written approval, executives of a significantly undercapitalized regulated entity may not receive bonuses or pay raises. In addition, FHFA may appoint a receiver or conservator for several specified causes related to financial difficulty or violations of law or regulation.

When a GSE becomes *critically undercapitalized*, receivership or conservatorship provisions apply. For example, FHFA must appoint itself as the receiver if a regulated entity's assets are (and have been for 60 days) less than its obligations to its creditors, or if the regulated entity has (for 60 days) not been generally paying its debts as they come due. Although both GSEs were technically adequately capitalized according to the March 2008 FHFA report, both firms were experiencing losses large enough to threaten continued solvency. In July 2008, Congress empowered Treasury to provide financial assistance to the GSEs, and the FHFA appointed itself conservator for both Fannie and Freddie in September 2008, before either GSE had failed to make timely payments on debt obligations.

FHFA may downgrade the capital classification of a regulated entity (1) whose conduct could rapidly deplete core or total capital, or (in the case of Fannie or Freddie) whose mortgage assets have declined significantly in value,

(2) that is determined (after notice and opportunity for a hearing) to be in an unsafe or unsound condition, or (3) that is engaging in an unsafe or unsound practice.

The SEC's Net Capital Rule

The SEC's net capital rule, set out in 17 CFR 240.15c3-1, imposes an "Aggregate Indebtedness Standard." No broker/dealer shall permit its aggregate indebtedness to all other persons to exceed 1500% of its net capital (or 800% of its net capital for 12 months after commencing business as a broker or dealer).[37] The 1500% (or 15-to-1) ratio of debt to liquid capital, is arithmetically equivalent to a 62/3% capital requirement.

To calculate liquid capital, SEC rules require that securities and other assets be given a "haircut" from their current market values (or face value, in the case of bonds), to cover the risk that the asset's value might decline before it could be sold. The haircut concept—the riskier the asset, the greater the haircut—is essentially the same as the standardized risk weights in the Basel Accords. For example, U.S. Treasury securities might have a lower haircut than municipal securities, which might have a lower haircut than corporate bonds, which in turn might have a lower haircut than common stock. Certain assets, such as unsecured receivables or securities for which no ready market exists, receive a haircut of 100%. The Dodd-Frank Act requires the SEC to set capital standards for major security-based swap dealers and major security-based swap participants.

CFTC Capital Requirements

Futures commission merchants (or FCMs, the futures equivalent of a securities broker/dealer) are subject to adjusted net capital requirements. Authority to enforce the capital rules is delegated by the CFTC to the National Futures Association (NFA), a self-regulatory organization created by Congress.

Each NFA member that is required to be registered with the CFTC as a futures commission merchant (member FCM) must maintain "Adjusted Net Capital" (as defined in CFTC Regulation 1.17) equal to or in excess of the greatest of

i. $500,000;
ii. For Member FCMs with less than $2,000,000 in Adjusted Net Capital, $6,000 for each remote location operated;
iii. For Member FCMs with less than $2,000,000 in Adjusted Net Capital, $3,000 for each associated person;
iv. For securities brokers and dealers, the amount of net capital specified by SEC regulations;
v. 8% of domestic and foreign domiciled customer and 4% of non-customer (excluding proprietary) risk maintenance margin/performance bond requirements for all domestic and foreign futures and options on futures contracts excluding the risk margin associated with naked long option positions;
vi. For Member FCMs with an affiliate that engages in foreign exchange (FX) transactions and that is authorized to engage in those transactions solely by virtue of its affiliation with a registered FCM, $7,500,000; or
vii. For Member FCMs that are counterparties to FX options, $5,000,000, except that FX Dealer Members must meet the higher requirement in Financial Requirements Section 11.[38]

The Dodd-Frank Act defines several categories of major derivatives participants and requires the CFTC to set capital standards for major security-based swap dealers and major security-based swap participants.

Foreign Exchange Markets

Buying and selling currencies is essential to foreign trade, and the exchange rate has major implications for a country's macroeconomic policy. Although the United States allows its currency to float, the foreign exchange market is not completely free because of the actions of central banks. For example, the central banks of other countries may seek to peg their currency to the dollar. The market is one of the largest in the world, with average daily foreign exchange turnover in excess of $4 trillion.[39] Federal Reserve monetary policies affect the value of the dollar (even if the Fed does not intentionally target the value of the dollar), but no agency is granted sole authority to regulate the mechanics of foreign exchange trading, except to the extent foreign exchange futures are offered on regulated exchanges.

Trading in currencies takes place between large global banks, central banks, hedge funds and other currency speculators, commercial firms involved in imports and exports, fund managers, and retail brokers. Currency trading is largely conducted in the over-the-counter market.

U.S. Treasury Securities

Like the foreign exchange market, there is no central exchange for the resale market for U.S. Treasuries, but there are a number of proprietary, computer-based transaction systems. Treasury securities were exempted from SEC regulation by the original securities laws of the 1930s and under the Volcker Rule in the Dodd-Frank Act. In 1993, following a successful corner of a Treasury bond auction by Salomon Brothers, Congress passed the Government Securities Act Amendments (P.L. 103-202), which required brokers and dealers in government securities that were not already registered with the SEC to register as government securities dealers. (Existing broker/dealer registrants were simply required to notify the SEC that they were in the government securities business.) Nevertheless, the government securities market remains much more lightly regulated than the corporate securities markets.

The primary market in Treasury securities, in which new debt instruments are sold to fund government operations, is monitored by the Federal Reserve Bank of New York (FRBNY). A principal channel for the distribution of new Treasuries is a group of firms called primary dealers, who purchase securities at auction for their own accounts and for their customers. The primary dealers are 19 commercial and investment banks, both foreign and domestic. The primary dealer list is maintained by the FRBNY, which also issues a list of practices that it expects primary dealers to comply with. FRBNY conducts auctions for the Treasury, but its relationship to the dealers is commercial, rather than providing prudential regulation.[40] The New York Fed does, however, collect certain data about primary dealers' transactions in government securities.

In March 2008, as part of its multifaceted attempt to supply liquidity to the financial system, the Federal Reserve established a Primary Dealer Credit Facility, to make short-term loans against a variety of collateral (including asset-backed and mortgage-backed securities) to the primary dealers.[41] This step attracted attention in part because the primary dealer group included investment banking firms of which the Fed had no regulatory authority.

Private Securities Markets

The securities laws mandate registration of, and extensive disclosures by, public securities issuers, but also provide for private sales of securities, which are not subject to disclosure requirements. Private placements of securities may only be offered to limited numbers of "accredited investors" who meet certain asset tests. (Most purchasers are life insurers and other institutional investors.) There are also restrictions on the resale of private securities.

The size of the private placement market is subject to considerable variation from year to year, but at times the value of securities sold privately exceeds what is sold into the public market. In recent decades, venture capitalists and private equity firms have come to play important roles in corporate finance. The former typically purchase interests in private firms, which may be sold later to the public, while the latter often purchase all the stock of publicly traded companies and take them private.

Appendix A. Capital Requirements: Provisions in Dodd-Frank

The Dodd-Frank Act includes numerous provisions that seek to strengthen capital requirements of banks and to extend capital regulatory approaches to certain non-bank financial firms and markets. The general thrust of these provisions is that systemically significant firms, derivatives trading platforms, and other financial market utilities should be required to hold extra capital to compensate for the risk that their failure might pose to the system at large. Title I requires banking regulators to establish minimum risk-based capital requirements and leverage requirements on a consolidated basis for depository institutions, depository holding companies, and firms designated by the Financial Stability Oversight Council (FSOC) as systemically significant. These requirements must be no lower than those that were set for depository institutions as of the date of enactment (July 2010). One example of the effect of this provision is that bank holding companies will no longer be able to include trust-preferred securities in Tier I capital. These requirements are phased in over time, and certain small firms are exempted.

Section 115(c) requires the Financial Stability Oversight Council to study the feasibility of implementing a contingent capital requirement for systemically significant firms. Contingent capital is debt that can be converted into equity by the issuing firm under certain circumstances. Following the study, if the FSOC recommends, the Fed may impose contingent capital requirements on systemically significant firms.

Section 165(j) requires the Federal Reserve to impose leverage limits on bank holding companies with assets over $50 billion and on the systemically important non-bank financial companies that it will supervise. When this section is implemented, such firms will be required to maintain a debt-to-equity ratio of no more than 15-to-1.

Title VI requires the federal banking regulators to make capital "requirements countercyclical, so that the amount of capital required to be maintained ... increases in times of economic expansion and decreases in times of economic contraction, consistent with ... safety and soundness."[42]

Table A-1. Capital Standards for Federally Regulated Depository Institutions

Agency	Capital Standard	Source
OCC (bank charters)	Minimum risk-based capital ratio of 8%. (The ratio measures bank capital against assets, with asset values risk-weighted, or adjusted on a scale of riskiness.) In addition, banks must maintain Tier 1 capital[a] in an amount equal to at least 3.0% of adjusted total assets. (A simple definition of Tier 1 capital is stockholders' equity, or the net worth of the institution.) The 3% total assets leverage ratio applies to the most highly rated banks, which are expected to have well-diversified risks, including no undue interest rate risk exposure, excellent control systems, good earnings, high asset quality, high liquidity, and well managed on-and off-balance sheet activities. In general, they should be considered strong banking organizations, with a rating of 1 under CAMELS[b] rating system of banks. For other banks, the minimum Tier 1 leverage ratio is 4%.	12 CFR §3.6 ("Minimum capital ratios")
FDIC	The FDIC requires institutions to maintain the same minimum leverage capital requirements (ratio of Tier 1 capital to assets) as the OCC, that is, 3% for the most highly rated institutions and 4% for others.	12 CFR §325.3 ("Minimum leverage capital requirement")
Federal Reserve	State banks that are members of the Federal Reserve System must meet an 8% risk-weighted capital standard, of which at least 4% must be Tier 1 capital (3% for strong banking institutions rated "1" under the CAMELS rating system of banks).	12 CFR §208.4, Regulation H ("Membership of State Banking Institutions in the Federal

Table A-1. (Continued)

Agency	Capital Standard	Source
	In addition, the Fed establishes levels of reserves that depository institutions are required to maintain as part of monetary policies. Changing reserve requirements could also affect potential bank lending in a way analogous to changing capital requirements. These reserves include vault cash (currency) or deposits at the nearest regional Federal Reserve branch, held against the bank's deposit liabilities, primarily checking, saving, and time deposits (CDs). The size of these reserves places a ceiling on the amount of deposits that financial institutions can have outstanding, and ties deposit liabilities to the amount of assets (loans) these institutions can acquire.	Reserve System") and 12 CFR §204.9 (Reserve requirements)
OCC (thrift charters)	Risk-based capital must be at least 8% of risk-weighted assets. Federal statute requires that thrift capital regulations be no less stringent than the OCC's regulations for banks. Tangible capital must exceed 1.5% of adjusted total assets. The leverage ratio (Tier 1 capital to assets) must be 4% of adjusted total assets (3% for thrifts with a composite CAMELS rating of 1).	12 CFR §167
NCUA	Credit unions must maintain a risk-based net worth of 7%, as a minimum to be considered well capitalized.	NCUA Regulations (Section 702, Subpart A)

Source: CRS from statutes and legislation.

[a] Tier 1 capital or core capital means the sum of common stockholders' equity, noncumulative perpetual preferred stock, and minority interests in consolidated subsidiaries, minus all intangible assets, minus identified losses, minus investments in certain financial subsidiaries, and minus the amount of the total adjusted carrying value of nonfinancial equity investments that is subject to a deduction from Tier 1 capital.

[b] See Appendix C for a broader discussion of the CAMELS rating system.

APPENDIX B. FORMS OF BANKING ORGANIZATIONS

The structure of banks can be complex. Currently, the regulator of a particular activity of a bank or its subsidiary depends in part on the activity of the subsidiary or its charter, as described previously. The following flow charts provide simplified representations of various bank structures. In some cases, the umbrella bank and its subsidiaries may have different regulators.

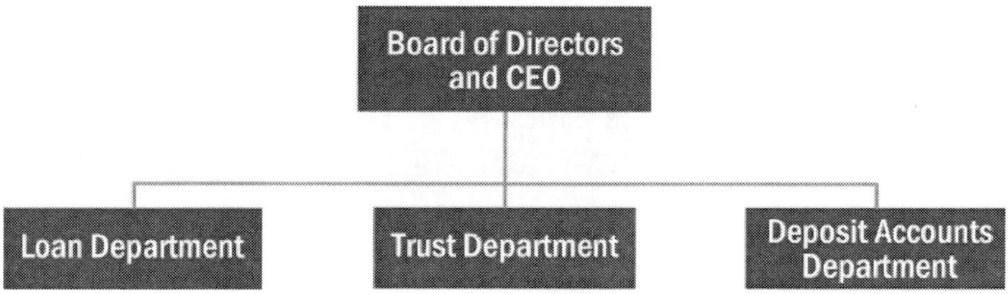

Source: The Congressional Research Service (CRS).

Figure B-1. National Bank.

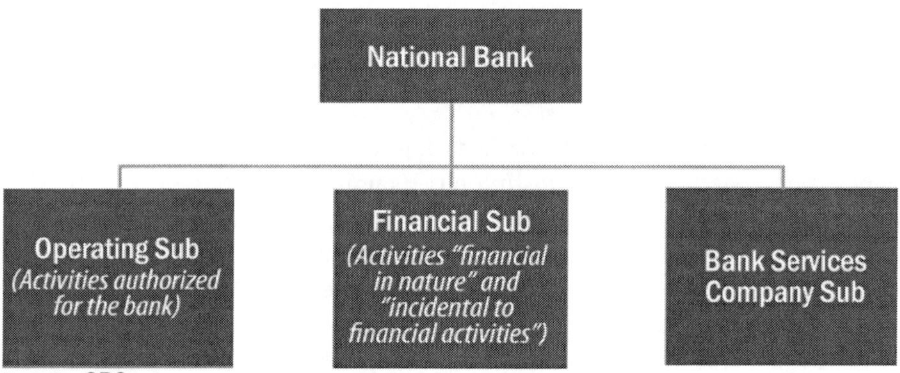

Source: CRS.

Figure B-2. National Bank and Subsidiaries.

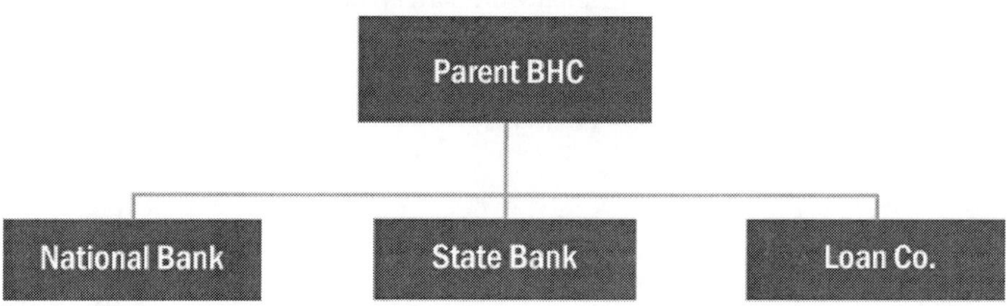

Source: CRS.

Figure B-3. Bank Holding Company.

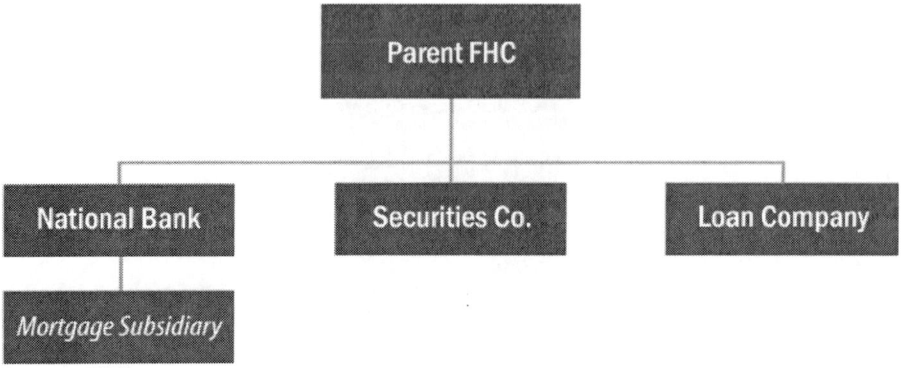

Source: CRS.

Figure B-4. Financial Holding Company.

APPENDIX C. BANK RATINGS: UFIRS AND CAMELS

Federal bank regulators conduct confidential assessments of covered banks. The Federal Financial Institutions Examination Council (FFIEC) helps coordinate the ratings system used by bank examiners so that there is some consistency to the examinations, although the ratings do take into account differences in bank size, sophistication, complexity of activities, and risk profile. The FFIEC adopted the Uniform Financial Institutions Rating System (UFIRS) in 1979. The system was revised in 1996 and is often referred to as the CAMELS rating system. CAMELS stands for Capital adequacy, Asset quality, Management, Earnings, Liquidity, and Sensitivity to market risk. These are measures used to evaluate the safety and soundness of banks. A description of the CAMELS system is found in the Comptrollers Handbook: Bank Supervision Process, provided by the Office of the Comptroller of the Currency (OCC).[43] Market factors can affect more than one category in the CAMELS ratings.

Capital Adequacy

This component assesses the level of capital held by the institution in relation to the risks that it takes. Capital adequacy can be affected by a number of factors, including changes in credit risk, market risk, and the institution's financial condition. Increases in problem assets would require increased capital. Capital adequacy is also supposed to reflect potential risks even if they are technically off of the bank's balance sheet.

Asset Quality

Asset quality refers to existing and potential credit risk associated with a bank's portfolio. Like capital adequacy, this component is supposed to reflect risk even if it is not technically on the bank's balance sheet. Asset quality can include changes in loan default rates, investment performance, exposure to counterparty risk, and all other risks that may affect the value or marketability of an institution's assets.

Management Capability

The governance of the bank, including management and board of directors, is assessed in relation to the nature and scope of the bank's activities. This rating is affected by the level and quality of management oversight. It also includes legal compliance, responsiveness to auditor recommendations, and similar issues.

Earnings Quantity and Quality

The rating of a bank's earnings takes into account current earnings and the sustainability of future earnings. Earnings that rely on favorable tax effects and nonrecurring events receive lower ratings. Similarly, inadequate controls for expenses can reduce the rating for earnings. Difficulties in forecasting and managing risks can also reduce the earnings rating.

Liquidity

Liquidity includes the ability of a bank to meet its expected funding needs. For a given institution size and complexity, this factor assesses the ability of the firm to fulfill its financial obligations in a timely manner. Liquidity refers to the ability to meet short-term funding needs without incurring excessive losses, which might occur if assets had to be sold at a steep discount in a time-pressure situation (or "fire sale"). Liquidity also includes assessments of specific financial categories, such as the trend and stability of deposits, and the expected ability to securitize and sell pools of assets.

Sensitivity to Market Risk

Market risk includes potential changes in the prices of financial assets, such as movements in interest rates, foreign exchange rates, commodity prices, and stock prices. The nature and scope of a bank's activities can affect the markets that it is exposed to; therefore, market risk is closely related to the other CAMELS factors. This rating takes into account management's ability to identify and manage the risks that can arise from the bank's trading activities in financial markets. It also takes into account interest rate risk from nontrading positions, such as any duration mismatch in loans held to maturity.

APPENDIX D. REGULATORY STRUCTURE BEFORE THE DODD-FRANK ACT

Regulatory Agency	Institutions Regulated	Emergency/Systemic Risk Powers	Other Notable Authority
Federal Reserve(The Fed)	Bank holding companies,[a] financial holding companies, state banks that are members of the Federal Reserve System, U.S. branches of foreign banks, foreign branches of U.S. banks	Lender of last resort to member banks (through discount window lending). In "unusual and exigent circumstances" the Fed may lend to "any individual, partnership, or corporation"	The Fed issues consumer protection regulations under various federal laws, including the Truth-in-Lending Act
Office of the Comptroller of the Currency (OCC)	National banks, U.S. federal branches of foreign banks		
Federal Deposit Insurance Corporation (FDIC)	Federally insured depository institutions, including state banks that are not members of the	After making a determination of systemic risk, the FDIC may invoke broad authority to use the deposit insurance	

Regulatory Agency	Institutions Regulated	Emergency/Systemic Risk Powers	Other Notable Authority
	Federal Reserve System	funds to provide an array of assistance to depository institutions	
Office of Thrift Supervision (OTS)	Federally chartered and insured thrift institutions, savings and loan holding companies		
National Credit Union Administration (NCUA)	Federally chartered or insured credit unions	Serves as a liquidity lender to credit unions experiencing liquidity shortfalls through the Central Liquidity Facility	Operates a deposit insurance fund for credit unions, the National Credit Union Share Insurance Fund (NCUSIF)
Securities and Exchange Commission (SEC)	Securities exchanges, brokers, and dealers; mutual funds; investment advisers. Registers corporate securities sold to the public	May unilaterally close markets or suspend trading strategies for limited periods	Authorized to set financial accounting standards which all publicly traded firms must use
Commodity Futures Trading Commission (CFTC)	Futures exchanges, brokers, pool operators, advisers	May suspend trading, order liquidation of positions, or raise margins in emergencies	
Federal Housing Finance Agency (FHFA)	Fannie Mae, Freddie Mac, and the Federal Home Loan Banks	Acting as conservator (since Sept. 2008) for Fannie and Freddie	

Source: CRS.

Note: Provisions in italics were repealed by Dodd-Frank.

[a] See Appendix B.

APPENDIX D: ACRONYMS

AICPA	American Institute of Certified Public Accountants
BIS	Bank for International Settlements
CAMELS	Capital Adequacy, Asset Quality, Management, Earnings, Liquidity, Sensitivity to Market Risk
CFTC	Commodity Futures Trading Commission

Appendix D. (Continued)

CSE	Consolidated Supervised Entities
DIF	Deposit Insurance Fund
EESA	Emergency Economic Stabilization Act
FASB	Financial Accounting Standards Board
FCM	Futures Commission Merchant
FDIC	Federal Deposit Insurance Corporation
FDICIA	The FDIC Improvement Act of 1991
FFIEC	Federal Financial Institution Examination Council
FHFA	Federal Housing Finance Agency
FHFB	Federal Housing Finance Board
FINRA	Financial Industry Regulatory Authority
FIRREA	The Financial Institutions Reform, Recovery, and Enforcement Act of 1989
FRB	Federal Reserve Board
FSOC	Financial Stability Oversight Council
FSLIC	Federal Savings and Loan Insurance Corporation
FX	Foreign Exchange
GLBA	Gramm-Leach-Bliley Act
GAAP	Generally Accepted Accounting Principles
GSE	Government-Sponsored Enterprise
NCUA	National Credit Union Administration
OCC	Office of the Comptroller of the Currency
OFHEO	Office of Federal Housing Enterprise Oversight
OFR	Office of Financial Research
OTS	Office of Thrift Supervision
PCS	Payment, Clearing, and Settlement Systems
PWG	President's Working Group on Capital Markets
SEC	Securities and Exchange Commission
SIPC	Securities Investor Protection Corporation
SRO	Self Regulatory Organization
UFIRS	Uniform Financial Institutions Rating System

Appendix E. Glossary of Terms

This glossary has been compiled from several earlier CRS reports, the CFTC and SIFMA websites, and other sources.

Affiliate—A corporate relationship of control. Two companies are affiliated when one owns all or a large part of another, or when both are controlled by a third (holding) company. (See "Subsidiary.") All subsidiaries are affiliates, but affiliates that are less than 50% controlled are usually not treated as subsidiaries.

Agency relationship—A business relationship of two parties in which one represents the other in transactions with third parties. The agent negotiates on behalf of the party actually at risk, who is known as the "principal." A commission goes to the agent who does not take on the risk of the transaction; the profit or loss goes to the principal.

Asset-backed security—A bond that represents a share in a pool of debt obligations or other assets. The holder is entitled to some part of the repayment flows from the underlying debt. (See "Securitization.") Mortgage-backed securities and asset backed commercial paper are examples of this.

Bank holding company—A business incorporated under state law, which controls through equity ownership ("holds") one or more banks and, often, other affiliates in financial services as allowed by its regulator, the Federal Reserve. On the federal level, these businesses are regulated through the Bank Holding Company Act.

Bank Holding Company Act—The federal statute under which the Federal Reserve regulates bank holding companies and financial holding companies (FHC). Besides the permissible financial activities enumerated in the Gramm-Leach-Bliley Act (P.L. 106-102), the law provides a mechanism between the Federal Reserve and the Department of the Treasury to decide what is an appropriate new financial activity for FHCs.

Basel Accords—International banking agreements coordinated through the Basel Committee on Bank Supervision (BCBS), which provides recommendations on banking regulations among participating countries.

Blue sky laws—State statutes that govern the offering and selling of securities.

Broker/dealer—An individual or firm that buys and sells securities for itself as well as for customers. Broker/dealers are registered with the Securities and Exchange Commission.

Bubble—Self-reinforcing process in which the price of an asset exceeds its fundamental value for a sustained period, often followed by a rapid price decline. Speculative bubbles are usually associated with a "bandwagon" effect in which speculators rush to buy the commodity (in the case of futures, "to take positions") before the price trend ends, and an even greater rush to sell the commodity (unwind positions) when prices reverse.

Capital requirements—Capital is the owners' stake in an enterprise. It is a critical line of defense when losses occur, both in banking and nonbanking enterprises. Capital requirements help assure that losses that might occur will accrue to the institution incurring them. In the case of banking institutions experiencing problems, capital also serves as a buffer against losses to the federal deposit insurance funds.

Charter conversion—Banking institutions may, with the approval of their regulators, switch their corporate form between: commercial bank or savings institution, National or State charter, and to stockholder ownership from depositor ownership. Various regulatory conditions may encourage switching.

Clearing Organization—An entity through which futures and other derivative transactions are cleared and settled. A clearing organization may be a division or affiliate of a particular exchange, or a freestanding entity. Also called a clearing house, multilateral clearing organization, or clearing association.

Collateralized debt obligation (CDO)—A bond created by the securitization of a pool of asset-backed securities.

Collateralized mortgage obligation (CMO)—A multiclass bond backed by a pool of mortgage pass-through securities or mortgage loans.

Commercial bank—A deposit-taking institution that can make commercial loans, accept checking accounts, and whose deposits are insured by the Federal Deposit Insurance Corporation. National banks are chartered by the Office of the Comptroller of the Currency; state banks, by the individual states.

Commodity Futures Modernization Act of 2000 (CFMA; P.L. 106-554, 114 Stat. 2763)— Overhauled the Commodity Exchange Act to create a flexible structure for the regulation of futures and options trading, and established a broad statutory exemption from regulation for OTC derivatives. Largely repealed by the Dodd-Frank Act.

Community financial institution—As provided for in the Gramm-Leach-Bliley Act, a member of the Federal Home Loan Bank System whose deposits are insured under the Federal Deposit Insurance Act and which has assets of less than $500 million (calculated according to provisions in the law, and in succeeding years to be adjusted for inflation). Such institutions may become members without meeting requirements with regard to the percentage of total assets that must be in residential mortgage loans and may borrow from the Federal Home Loan Banks for small business and agriculture.

Conservatorship—When an insolvent financial institution is reorganized by a regulator with the intent to restoring it to an ongoing business.

Counterparty—The opposite party in a bilateral agreement, contract, or transaction, such as a swap.

Credit Default Swap (CDS)—A tradeable contract in which one party agrees to pay another if a third party experiences a credit event, such as default on a debt obligation, bankruptcy, or credit rating downgrade.

Credit Risk—The risk that a borrower will fail to repay a loan in full, or that a derivatives counterparty will default.

Credit union—A nonprofit financial cooperative of individuals with one or more common bonds (such as employment, labor union membership, or residence in the same neighborhood). May be state or nationally chartered. Credit unions accept deposits of members' savings and transaction balances in the form of share accounts, pay dividends (interest) on them out of earnings, and primarily provide consumer credit to members. The federal regulator for credit unions is the National Credit Union Administration (NCUA).

Dealer—An individual or financial firm engaged in the purchase and sale of securities and commodities such as metals, foreign exchange, etc., for its own account and at its own risk as principal (see broker). Commercial banks are typically limited to acting as dealers in specified high-quality debt obligations, such as those of the federal government.

Depository institution—Customarily refers to commercial banks, savings institutions, and credit unions, since traditionally the greater part of their funding has been in the form of deposits. Deposits are a customer's funds placed with an institution according to agreed-upon terms and conditions and represent a credit to the depositor.

Derivatives—Financial contracts whose value is linked to the price of an underlying commodity or financial variable (such as an interest rate, currency price, or stock index). Ownership of a derivative does not require the holder to actually buy or sell the underlying interest. Derivatives are used by hedgers, who seek to shift risk to others, and speculators, who can profit if they can successfully forecast price trends. Examples include futures contracts, options, and swaps.

Discount window—Figurative term for the Federal Reserve facility for extending credit directly to eligible depository institutions. It may be used to relieve temporary cash shortages at banks and other depository institutions. Borrowers are expected to have tried to borrow elsewhere first and must provide collateral as security for loans. The term derives from the practice whereby bankers would come to a Reserve Bank teller window to obtain credit in the early days of the Federal Reserve System.

Dual banking system—The phrase refers to the fact that banks may be either federally or state-chartered. In the case of state-chartered banks, the state is the primary regulator; for national banks, the Office of the Comptroller of the Currency is the primary regulator.

Electronic fund transfer (EFT) systems—A variety of systems and technologies for transferring funds electronically rather than by paper check.

Exchange—A central marketplace with established rules and regulations where buyers and sellers meet to trade futures and options contracts or securities.

Federal Home Loan Banks—Twelve regional member-owned federally sponsored organizations that extend credit to their member banking institutions, largely to finance mortgages made to homeowners. The 12 FHLBs make up a single government-sponsored enterprise.

Federal safety net—A broad term referring to protection of banking institutions through deposit insurance, discount window credit, other lender of last resort support, and certain forms of regulations to reduce risk. Commercial and industrial companies generally lack any of these cushions against loss.

Financial businesses—In discussions about financial services modernization, usually refers to commercial banks and savings institutions, securities firms, and insurance companies and agents, as contrasted with commercial and industrial firms.

Financial holding company—A form of bank holding company authorized by the GrammLeach-Bliley Act that may control one or more banks, securities firms, and insurance companies.

Financial institution—An enterprise that uses its funds chiefly to purchase financial assets such as loans and debt securities, as opposed to tangible property. Financial institutions are differentiated by the manner in which they invest their funds: in loans, bonds, stocks, or some combination; as well as by their sources of funds. Depository financial institutions are differentiated in that they may accept deposits which are federally insured against loss to the depositor. Nondepository financial institutions such as life and property/casualty insurance companies, pension funds, and mutual funds obtain funds through other types of receipts, whose values may fluctuate with market conditions.

Financial subsidiary—Under the Gramm-Leach-Bliley Act, both national and state-chartered banks are authorized to form financial subsidiaries to engage in activities that would not otherwise be permitted within the bank itself, subject to certain limits. Besides the permissible financial activities enumerated in P.L. 106-102, the law provides a mechanism between the U.S. Department of the Treasury and the Federal Reserve to decide what is an appropriate new financial activity for a financial subsidiary.

Firewalls—Barriers to the flow of capital, information, management, and other resources among business units owned by a common entity. In case of financial distress of one operation ("fire"), the "walls" are intended to prevent the spread of loss to the other units—especially to banking units. Example: losses in a securities subsidiary of a holding company could not be covered by any of the holding company's bank subsidiaries.

Foreign bank—Banks and their holding companies headquartered in other countries may have a variety of financial operations in the United States: U.S.-chartered subsidiary banks, agencies, branches, and representative offices. Their primary federal regulator is the Federal Reserve, under the International Banking Act of 1978 as amended. States and the Office of the Comptroller of the Currency may also regulate them, depending on whether they have a state or federal charter.

Forward Contract—A cash transaction in which a buyer and seller agree upon delivery of a specified quality and quantity of goods at a specified future date.

Functional regulation—Regulatory arrangements based on activity ("function") rather than organizational structure. The Gramm-Leach-Bliley Act called for more functional regulation than in the past.

Futures Contract—An agreement to purchase or sell a commodity for delivery in the future: (1) at a price that is determined at initiation of the contract; (2) that obligates each party to the contract to fulfill the contract at the specified price; (3) that is used to assume or shift price risk; and (4) that may be satisfied by delivery or offset.

Glass-Steagall Act—Part of the Banking Act of 1933; divided the commercial and investment banking industries. The Gramm-Leach-Bliley Act repealed two sections of the act dealing with the relationship between banks and securities firms.

Government-sponsored enterprise (GSE)—GSEs are private companies with government charters. Government sponsorship typically gives them a funding advantage over purely private competitors, while their charters restrict the kinds of businesses they may conduct.

Gramm-Leach-Bliley Act of 1999—P.L. 106-102, also known as the Financial Services Modernization Act, authorized increased affiliations between banks, securities firms, and insurers. Permitted the establishment of financial holding companies, under the regulation of the Federal Reserve. Also addressed privacy protection for consumers' financial data.

Haircut—In computing the value of assets for purposes of capital, segregation, or margin requirements, a percentage reduction from the stated value (e.g., book value or market value) to account for possible declines in value that may occur before assets can be liquidated.

Hedge funds—Hedge funds are essentially unregulated mutual funds. They are pools of invested money that buy and sell stocks and bonds and many other assets, including precious metals, commodities, foreign currencies, and derivatives (contracts whose prices are derived from those of other financial instruments). Hedge funds are limited to qualified investors with high net worth.

Hedging—Investing with the intention of reducing the impact of adverse movements in interest rates, commodities, or securities prices. Typically, the hedging instrument gains value as the hedged item loses value, and vice versa.

Insolvent—A firm whose liabilities exceed its assets.

Institutional regulation—Regulation that is institution-specific as contrasted with activity-specific (see functional regulation).

Investment bank—A financial intermediary, active in the securities business. Investment banking functions include underwriting (marketing newly registered securities to individual or institutional investors), counseling regarding merger and acquisition proposals, brokerage services, advice on corporate financing, and proprietary trading.

Investment bank holding company—A holding company for securities firms authorized under the Gramm-Leach-Bliley Act. Such holding companies are subject to regulation by the Securities and Exchange Commission.

Issuer—A person or entity (including a company or bank) that offers securities for sale. The issuing of securities, where the proceeds accrue to the issuer, is distinct from the secondary, or resale, market, where securities are traded among investors.

Lender of last resort—Governmental lender that acts as the ultimate source of credit in the financial system. In the United States, the Federal Reserve has this role.

Leverage—In derivatives markets, leverage (or "gearing") often refers to the ability to control large dollar amounts of a commodity or security with a comparatively small amount of capital. In banking, the term leverage is often used to describe the amount of a bank's assets that are funded with debt rather than equity. In banking, leverage is typically the ratio of lending to equity.

Limited-purpose bank—Although generally commercial firms may not conduct a banking business, some exceptions exist. Examples: Nonbank banks are banks that either accept deposits or make commercial loans but cannot do both. Such banks grew up through a loophole in the law, which was closed by the Competitive Equality Banking Act of 1987 (CEBA). Credit card banks conduct credit card operations. Industrial loan companies in a few states may offer restricted banking services.

Liquidity—The ability to trade an asset quickly without significantly affecting its price, or the condition of a market with many buyers and sellers present. Also, the ability of a person or firm to access credit markets.

Liquidity risk—The possibility that the market for normally-liquid assets will suddenly dry up, leaving firms unable to convert assets into cash. Also, the risk that other firms will refuse to extend credit on any terms to a firm that is perceived as distressed.

Market risk—The risk that the price of a tradeable security or asset will decline, resulting in a loss to the holder.

Merchant banker—A European style investment banker concentrating on corporate deals, in which it may invest its own funds.

Money market mutual fund (MMF)—A form of mutual fund that pools funds of individuals and other investors for investment in high-grade, short-term debt and bank deposits paying market rates of return. Examples of these money market instruments include U.S. Treasury bills, certificates of deposit, and commercial paper. In addition to the investment features, most MMFs offer check-writing redemption features.

Moral hazard—The tendency of people to take more risks once another party has agreed to provide protection. Regulatory interventions to bail out failing firms are often said to create moral hazard, on the assumption that others will expect to be saved from their mistakes, too.

Mortgage-backed security (MBS)—A bond backed by a pool of mortgage loans. The bondholders receive a share of the interest and principal payments on the underlying mortgages. The cash flows may be divided among different classes of bonds, called tranches.

Mutual fund—An investing company that pools the funds of individuals and other investors, and uses them to purchase large amounts of debt or equity obligations of businesses and sometimes debt obligations of governments. The owners of the mutual fund hold proportional shares in the entire pool of securities in which a fund invests. Owners pay taxes on their distributions from a fund; the mutual fund itself is not normally subject to federal or state income taxation.

Naked option—The sale of a call or put option without holding an equal and opposite position in the underlying instrument.

Operational risk—The possibility that a financial institution will suffer losses from a failure to process transactions properly, from accounting mistakes, from rogue traders or other forms of insider fraud, or from other causes arising inside the institution.

Over-the-counter (OTC)—Trading that does not occur on a centralized exchange or trading facility. OTC transactions can occur electronically or over the telephone.

Ponzi Scheme—Named after Charles Ponzi, a man with a remarkable criminal career in the early 20th century, the term has been used to describe pyramid arrangements whereby an enterprise makes payments to investors from the proceeds of a later investment rather than from profits of the underlying business venture, as the investors expected, and gives investors the impression that a legitimate profit-making business or investment opportunity exists, where in fact it is a mere fiction.

Prompt corrective action (PCA)—A framework of bank regulation in which banks with insufficient capital must undertake remedial action to improve their capital positions. In the United States, the PCA framework has five categories of bank capitalization. Financially troubled banks are required to take prompt action as directed by the relevant agencies to remedy identified deficiencies.

Receivership—When an insolvent financial institution is taken over with the intent to liquidate its assets.

Regulatory Arbitrage—If different contract types or firm charters can be used to achieve similar ends, but have different regulatory treatment, then regulatory arbitrage refers to attempts to receive the least burdensome regulatory treatment for a given activity. In economics, arbitrage is the practice of taking advantage of a price difference between two or more markets.

Resolution Trust Corporation (RTC)—The agency set up to resolve savings and loans declared failed beginning in 1989. Between 1989 and mid-1995, the Resolution Trust Corporation closed or otherwise resolved 747 thrifts with total assets of $394 billion.

Repurchase Agreement (Repo)—A contract in which one party sells a contract (typically a bond or other debt contract) to buyer, with a commitment to repurchase the contract on a future date at a specified price. In economics, repurchase agreements have similar characteristics to collateralized lending.

Savings association—A savings and loan association, mutual savings bank, or federal savings bank, whose primary function has traditionally been to encourage personal saving (thrift) and home buying through mortgage lending. In recent years, such institutions' charters have been expanded to allow them to provide commercial loans and a broader range of consumer financial services. The federal regulator for most savings associations is the Office of Thrift Supervision. Also known as savings and loans, thrifts, and mutual savings banks.

Securities Investor Protection Corporation (SIPC)—A private nonprofit membership corporation set up under federal law to provide financial protection for the customers of failed brokers and/or dealers. SIPC is a liquidator; it has no supervisory or regulatory responsibilities for its members, nor is it authorized to bail out or in other ways assist a failing firm.

Securitization—The process of transforming a cash flow, typically from debt repayments, into a new marketable security. Holders of the securitized instrument receive interest and principal payments as the underlying loans are repaid. Types of loans that are frequently securitized are home mortgages, credit card receivables, student loans, small business loans, and car loans.

Self-regulatory organizations (SROs)—National securities or futures exchanges, national securities or futures associations, clearing agencies and the Municipal Securities Rulemaking Board are all authorized to make and enforce rules governing market participants. The respective federal regulatory agency has authority in connection with SROs and may require them to adopt or modify their rules. Examples of SROs in the securities industry include the Financial Industry Regulatory Authority (FINRA), and the New York Stock Exchange.

Shadow banking—The funding of loans through firms that do not have bank charters, through securities markets, or the funding of banks with sources other than deposits. Often, the term shadow banking is used to describe financial intermediation with at least one deviation from a model in which banks raise all of their funds from sources with government guarantees (such as deposit insurance) and banks have access to emergency government lending facilities, such as the Federal Reserve's discount window.

Special-purpose entities (SPEs)—Also referred to as off–balance-sheet arrangements, SPEs are legal entities created to perform a specific financial function or transaction. They isolate financial risk from the sponsoring institution and provide less-expensive financing. The assets, liabilities, and cash flows of an SPE do not appear on the sponsoring institution's books.

Speculation—A venture or undertaking of an enterprising nature, especially one involving considerable financial risk on the chance of unusual profit.

State regulation—Under the dual system of bank regulation, states as well as the federal government may charter, regulate, and supervise depository institutions. States are the primary regulators in the insurance field. States also have authority over securities companies, mortgage lending companies, personal finance companies, and other types of companies offering financial services.

Structured debt—Debt that has been customized for the buyer, often by incorporating complex derivatives.

Subordinated debt—Debt over which senior debt takes priority. In the event of bankruptcy, subordinated debt holders receive payment only after senior debt claims are paid in full.

Subsidiary—A company whose controlling shares are owned 50% or more by another ("parent") corporation. Like companies with less than 50% ownership, it is an affiliate of the controlling company. A subsidiary is usually consolidated for regulatory and reporting purposes with its parent.

Swap—The exchange of one asset or liability for a similar asset or liability for the purpose of lengthening or shortening maturities, or otherwise shifting risks. For example, parties could exchange a fixed interest rate stream of income for a floating rate stream of income, or a stream of income based on one currency's exchange rate for a stream of income based on another currency's exchange rate.

Systemic Risk—The term *systemic risk* does not have a single, agreed-upon definition. Some define systemic risk as the risk an institution faces that it cannot diversify against. In other circumstances, systemic risk is defined as the risk that the linkages between institutions may affect the financial system as a whole, through a dynamic sometimes referred to as contagion.

Thrift holding company—Also known as a savings and loan holding company, a business that controls one or more savings associations. These holding companies are regulated under the Home Owners' Loan Act by the Office of Thrift Supervision.

Too-big-to-fail doctrine—An implicit regulatory policy holding that very large financial institutions must be rescued by the government, because their failure would destabilize the entire financial system. (See "Moral Hazard.")

Umbrella supervision—The term applied to comprehensive regulation of a holding company and its parts by one or more holding company regulator(s).

Underwriter—For securities markets, see investment bankers. For insurance, underwriters are the life, health and property-casualty companies that receive premiums and pay off losses and other risks as they occur. The underwriters bear the risks of losses and expenses exceeding receipts.

Unitary thrift holding company (UTHC)—A holding company that owns a single thrift institution. A distinction between UTHCs and other thrift holding companies has been that a UTHC could be involved in any lines of business, whereas the others have been restricted to certain activities primarily financial in nature. The Gramm-Leach-Bliley Act limits the commercial activities and affiliations of new UTHCs.

Universal bank—An organizational model typical of some foreign countries whereby a bank can exist as an operating enterprise and own directly a variety of other businesses. (See "Subsidiary.") It contrasts with the banking model typical in the United States where the parent holding company owns several different businesses, all structurally separate. (See "Affiliate.") In practice, the two approaches are not exclusive.

Volcker Rule—Section 619 of the Dodd-Frank Act, which prohibits insured depository banks and their affiliated firms from engaging in proprietary trading or affiliating with hedge funds.

End Notes

[1] A fifth agency, the Office of Thrift Supervision (OTS), was abolished in 2010, and its responsibilities were spread among other agencies. Its prudential regulation of thrift depositories was transferred to the Office of the Comptroller of the Currency. Its prudential regulation of thrift holding companies was transferred to the Federal Reserve.

[2] The Federal Reserve also provides prudential regulation to certain nonbank financial companies and financial-market utilities that are designated as systemic.

[3] Although the distinction between prudence-based regulators and disclosure-based regulators may be true in general, bank regulators can regulate the disclosures of their chartered firms and securities and derivatives regulators do have some prudential responsibilities. For example, Section 731 of the Dodd-Frank Act instructs derivatives regulators to set capital requirements for major swap participants.

[4] The term agency is being used to describe the functional relationship and does not imply any contractual obligation.

[5] The term agent is being used to describe the functional relationship, not any contractual obligations.

[6] See, e.g., U.S. Department of the Treasury, Blueprint for a Modern Financial Regulatory Structure, March 2008, which called for a three-agency structure: a systemic risk regulator, a markets supervisor, and a consumer regulator.

[7] "Competition Among Bank Regulators," John Weinberg, Economic Quarterly, Fall 2002, available at http://www.richmondfed.org/publications/research/economic_quarterly/2002/fall/pdf/weinberg.pdf.

[8] Illustrations of several forms of depository organization are presented in Appendix B.

[9] Historically, "banks" also referred to firms with special charters that issued debt, which often circulated as currency. The Bank of England had been granted a monopoly on this form of banking (note issue), which was determined not to extend to depository banking in the nineteenth century.

[10] As described in a Wall Street Journal article, available at http://online.wsj.com/article/SB10000872396390444433504577649971326432962.html.

[11] This report will not track the ultimate fate of the ice cream shop. The owner reportedly changed the name to remove the word bank. Regulatory interaction is likely to be ongoing. For example, see "Pittsburgh ice cream bank owner says regulators are backing off," WTAE News, available at http://www.wtae.com/news/local/allegheny/Pittsburgh-icecream-bank-owner-says-regulators-are-backing-off/-/10927008/19522712/-/asy08i/-/index.html.

[12] Regulatory uses of "capital" include more specific definitions and classifications.

[13] See CRS Report R42744, U.S. Implementation of the Basel Capital Regulatory Framework, by Darryl E. Getter.

[14] Bank for International Settlements, "About the Basel Committee," January 23, 2013, available at http://www.bis.org/ bcbs/about.htm.

[15] Section 135 of the Emergency Economic Stabilization Act of 2008 (EESA; P.L. 110-343).

[16] CRS Report R41718, Federal Deposit Insurance for Banks and Credit Unions, by Darryl E. Getter.

[17] FDICIA created a new Section 13(c)(4) of the Federal Deposit Insurance Act, 12 USC §1823(c)(4)(G).

[18] FDIC, "FDIC Announces Plan to Free Up Bank Liquidity," press release, October 14, 2008, http://www.fdic.gov/ news/news/press/2008/pr08100.html.

[19] For more detail, see CRS Report R41384, The Dodd-Frank Wall Street Reform and Consumer Protection Act: Systemic Risk and the Federal Reserve, by Marc Labonte.

[20] A counter example would be SEC's net capital rule as discussed below in "The SEC's Net Capital Rule."

[21] See CRS Report RL34420, Bear Stearns: Crisis and "Rescue" for a Major Provider of Mortgage-Related Products, by Gary Shorter.

[22] See CRS Report RL34427, Financial Turmoil: Federal Reserve Policy Responses, by Marc Labonte.

[23] SEC, "Holding Company Supervision Program Description: Consolidated Supervised Entities ("CSEs")," http://www.sec.gov/divisions/marketreg/hcsupervision.htm.

[24] The Market Reform Act of 1990 permits the SEC to collect certain financial information from unregulated affiliates of broker/dealers, under the Broker-Dealer Risk Assessment Program. The impetus for the CSE program was a European Union requirement that investment banks operating in Europe be subject to consolidated financial supervision.

[25] Some argue that CSE allowed the investment banks to hold less capital and increase their leverage. For two views on this issue, see Stephen Labaton, "Agency's '04 Rule Let Banks Pile Up New Debt, and Risk," New York Times, October 3, 2008, p. A1, and Testimony of SEC Chairman Christopher Cox, House Oversight and Government Reform Committee, October 23, 2008. (Response to question from Rep. Christopher Shays.)

[26] By becoming bank holding companies, Morgan Stanley and Goldman Sachs placed themselves under Federal Reserve regulation, presumably to signal to the markets that their financial condition was being monitored and to gain access to the Fed's lending facilities.

[27] SEC, "Chairman Cox Announces End of Consolidated Supervised Entities Program," press release 2008-230.

[28] For more on GSEs and their regulation, see CRS Reports CRS Report R40800, GSEs and the Government's Role in Housing Finance: Issues for the 113th Congress, by N. Eric Weiss.

[29] See CRS Report R42760, Fannie Mae's and Freddie Mac's Financial Status: Frequently Asked Questions, by N. Eric Weiss.

[30] See CRS Report R41338, The Dodd-Frank Wall Street Reform and Consumer Protection Act: Title X, The Consumer Financial Protection Bureau, by David H. Carpenter. CRS Report R42615, A Brief Overview of Actions Taken by the Consumer Financial Protection Bureau (CFPB) in Its First Year, by Sean M. Hoskins.

[31] See CRS Report R41384, The Dodd-Frank Wall Street Reform and Consumer Protection Act: Systemic Risk and the Federal Reserve, by Marc Labonte.

[32] P.L. 95-630, 92 STAT. 3641.

[33] Executive Order 12631, March 18, 1988, 53 FR 9421.

[34] President's Working Group on Financial Markets, "Policy Statement on Financial Market Developments," March 2008, http://www.ustreas.gov/press/releases/reports/pwgpolicystatemktturmoil_03122008.pdf.

[35] Securities and Exchange Commission, "President's Working Group Report on Money Market Fund Reform," Release No. IC-29497; File No. 4-619, available at http://www.sec.gov/rules/other/2010/ic-29497.pdf.

[36] See Sections 1142 and 1143 of the Housing and Economic Recovery Act of 2008, P.L. 110-289.

[37] This is an example of the SEC regulation for the risk that a firm takes, as alluded to in the description of the SEC.

[38] National Futures Association, NFA Manual/Rules, Section 7001, http://www.nfa.futures.org/nfaManual/ manualFinancial.asp#fins1.

[39] Bank for International Settlements, Triennial Central Bank Survey of Foreign Exchange and Derivatives Market Activity, September 2010, http://www.bis.org/publ/rpfxf10t.htm.

[40] See http://www.newyorkfed.org/aboutthefed/fedpoint/fed02.html.

[41] Federal Reserve Bank of New York, "Federal Reserve Announces Establishment of Primary Dealer Credit Facility," Press Release, March 16, 2008, http://www.newyorkfed.org/ news events/news/markets/2008/rp080316.html.

[42] Dodd-Frank Act, Section 616.

[43] The Comptrollers handbooks are occasionally updated. The handbook for the Bank Supervision Process can be found at http://www.occ.gov/handbook/banksup.pdf.

INDEX

#

20th century, 31, 96

A

access, 4, 22, 25, 32, 36, 44, 47, 48, 68, 95, 98, 101
accounting, 24, 54, 59, 69, 74, 87, 96
accounting standards, 54, 69, 74, 87
age, 37
agencies, vii, 30, 35, 37, 39, 49, 50, 52, 54, 57, 63, 64, 67, 69, 75, 93, 96, 97, 100
agriculture, 91
appraisals, 63
arbitrage, 3, 32, 50, 97
Asia, 30
assessment, 65, 66
assets, 5, 10, 11, 12, 13, 14, 15, 16, 18, 19, 21, 22, 23, 24, 25, 27, 28, 30, 31, 33, 39, 44, 48, 54, 55, 59, 61, 62, 66, 69, 70, 73, 76, 77, 81, 82, 84, 85, 86, 89, 91, 92, 94, 95, 96, 97, 98
asymmetry, 15
audit, 75
authority(s), 18, 19, 23, 25, 36, 37, 38, 39, 41, 49, 50, 52, 53, 54, 56, 58, 61, 63, 64, 65, 66, 68, 69, 70, 71, 72, 73, 74, 78, 79, 86, 97, 98

B

bail, 95, 97
balance sheet, 24, 29, 30, 45, 59, 60, 66, 81, 85
ban, 56
bank charter, 5, 7, 8, 22, 32, 41, 75, 81, 98
bank debt, 65
bank failure, 44, 58, 65
bank holding companies, 53, 66, 71, 80, 81, 89, 101
Bank of England, 100
bankers, 43, 92
Banking Act of 1933, 94
banking sector, vii, 2, 3, 7, 9, 11, 12, 17
bankruptcy, 3, 21, 23, 27, 32, 70, 91, 98
base, 43, 66, 71
benefits, 38, 41
bondholders, 96
bonds, 9, 13, 14, 22, 31, 37, 51, 68, 77, 91, 93, 94, 96
bonuses, 76
borrowers, vii, 5, 8, 13, 15, 19, 22, 25, 35, 42, 43, 56, 59
business model, 5, 13, 23, 36, 43, 60
businesses, 55, 60, 61, 89, 92, 94, 96, 99
buyer(s), 14, 15, 45, 47, 92, 93, 95, 97, 98

C

capital adequacy, 61, 75, 85
cash, 14, 15, 56, 59, 82, 92, 93, 95, 96, 97, 98
cash flow, 59, 96, 97, 98
category a, 39
central bank, 78, 79
certificates of deposit, 27, 95
CFR, 77, 81, 82
challenges, 26, 27
Chicago, 31, 51
Chicago Mercantile Exchange, 51
circulation, 64
City, 31
classes, 12, 14, 15, 18, 33, 36, 51, 56, 69, 96
classification, 76
clients, 46, 50, 62
collateral, 2, 8, 15, 16, 19, 20, 21, 23, 30, 39, 47, 56, 62, 63, 79, 92
commercial, 2, 4, 8, 9, 24, 27, 33, 42, 43, 45, 48, 60, 64, 79, 89, 90, 91, 92, 94, 95, 97, 99
commercial bank, 9, 42, 43, 45, 64, 90, 91, 92
commodity, 46, 51, 54, 71, 86, 90, 91, 93, 95
commodity futures, 51
commodity markets, 46
communication, 39
community, 43, 58, 67
compensation, 71
competitive advantage, 44
competitiveness, 74
competitors, 94
complexity, 84, 85
compliance, 58, 63, 64, 70, 75, 85
composition, 12, 39, 44, 59
computer, 79
computing, 94
conception, 6
conference, 31, 32
Congress, vii, 1, 3, 23, 28, 29, 30, 33, 35, 37, 65, 69, 70, 71, 73, 74, 76, 77, 79, 101
consolidation, 49
constituents, 37
consumer protection, 26, 37, 72, 75, 86
consumers, vii, 23, 35, 51, 56, 63, 73, 94
controversial, 56
controversies, 49
cooperation, 61
coordination, 32, 39, 73, 74
corporate finance, 80
corporate governance, 68
cost, 16, 60
counseling, 94
credit market, 95
credit rating, 25, 26, 91
creditors, 18, 22, 23, 32, 36, 48, 66, 76
crises, 50, 65
currency, 64, 78, 79, 82, 91, 98, 100
customer relations, 63
customers, 56, 60, 69, 79, 90, 97

D

database, 27
debentures, 12
debts, 8, 42, 45, 76
deduction, 82
deficiencies, 96
Department of Education, 31
Department of Justice, 52
Department of the Treasury, 49, 64, 89
depository banks, vii, 1, 4, 56, 57, 63, 99
depository institutions, 53, 54, 64, 65, 66, 73, 75, 80, 82, 86, 92, 98
deposits, 3, 5, 7, 8, 9, 13, 14, 21, 27, 29, 40, 42, 43, 47, 48, 56, 65, 66, 67, 82, 86, 90, 91, 93, 95, 98
deregulation, 31
derivatives, 13, 26, 36, 39, 41, 42, 50, 57, 59, 64, 68, 71, 72, 75, 78, 80, 90, 91, 94, 95, 98, 100
developed nations, 37
deviation, 98
directors, 76, 85
disclosure, 2, 4, 17, 28, 36, 38, 49, 68, 80, 100
discrimination, 43, 52

disposition, 26
distortions, 46
distress, 16
distribution, 32, 79
diversification, 28, 58
diversity, 4, 17, 28, 29
Dodd-Frank Wall Street Reform and Consumer Protection Act, 101

E

earnings, 43, 81, 85, 91
economic boom, 61
economic downturn, 62
economic growth, 37
economic policy, 43, 58, 59, 62, 65, 67
economic problem, vii, 4
economics, 97
education, 37
EESA, 88, 100
eligibility criteria, 23
emergency, vii, 1, 2, 3, 4, 19, 22, 23, 24, 25, 27, 41, 44, 47, 56, 65, 98
Emergency Economic Stabilization Act (EESA), 33, 88, 100
employees, 58
employment, 52, 91
encouragement, 61
enforcement, 36, 52, 59, 64, 68, 73
environment(s), 60, 62
equity(s), 12, 18, 42, 45, 59, 72, 76, 80, 81, 82, 89, 95, 96
Europe, 56, 101
European style, 95
European Union, 101
evidence, 58
evolution, 51
examinations, 28, 57, 63, 64, 68, 84
exchange rate, 28, 78, 98
execution, 54, 71
Executive Order, 101
expertise, 58, 73
exports, 79
exposure, 14, 18, 58, 59, 81, 85
external financing, 24
externalities, 32

F

facilitators, 68
factories, 12
faith, 65
Fannie Mae, 13, 22, 26, 31, 32, 33, 36, 55, 72, 76, 87, 101
FAS, 24, 33
FDIC, 2, 15, 22, 23, 29, 30, 32, 37, 38, 40, 53, 57, 64, 65, 66, 69, 73, 75, 81, 86, 88, 100
fear(s), 15, 45, 62
federal banking regulators, 75, 81
federal government, 31, 65, 91, 98
Federal Housing Finance Agency (FHFA), 23, 36, 38, 39, 55, 72, 76, 87, 88
federal law, 86, 97
Federal Reserve, 2, 10, 14, 19, 20, 21, 23, 24, 30, 31, 32, 36, 37, 38, 40, 53, 54, 57, 64, 66, 67, 70, 71, 72, 74, 78, 79, 81, 82, 86, 88, 89, 92, 93, 95, 100, 101, 102
Federal Reserve Board, 20, 38, 66, 88
FHFA, 36, 72, 73, 76, 88
financial condition, 16, 26, 39, 68, 70, 84, 101
financial crisis, vii, 1, 3, 9, 11, 15, 19, 20, 21, 24, 25, 28, 29, 32, 36, 50, 63, 65, 66, 75
financial data, 72, 94
financial difficulty, 76
financial distress, 93
financial firms, vii, 1, 16, 37, 42, 45, 50, 53, 67, 74, 80
financial innovation, 4, 56
financial instability, vii, 1, 4, 19, 23, 32, 35, 46, 62
financial institutions, 12, 13, 14, 16, 32, 37, 48, 52, 66, 68, 72, 82, 93, 99
financial intermediaries, 16, 17, 18, 19, 73
financial markets, vii, 11, 12, 31, 32, 35, 37, 45, 49, 67, 86
financial problems, vii, 1
financial regulation, 3, 41, 49, 50, 56

Financial Services Authority, 50
financial soundness, 72
financial stability, 2, 3, 39, 44, 53, 66, 74
financial support, 36
financial system, 4, 5, 11, 16, 19, 31, 37, 40, 42, 49, 50, 51, 53, 60, 67, 74, 79, 95, 99
fixed rate, 13
flaws, 48
fluctuations, 15, 19
food, 52
food service employee, 52
forecasting, 85
foreclosure, 16, 27
foreign banks, 53, 66, 86
foreign exchange, 78, 79, 86, 91
foreign exchange market, 78, 79
formation, 73
fraud, 51, 68, 69, 71, 96
Freddie Mac, 13, 26, 31, 32, 36, 55, 72, 76, 87, 101
FSB, 11, 20, 29, 30, 31
funding, 3, 9, 12, 16, 19, 24, 27, 29, 31, 47, 65, 85, 91, 94, 98
funds, 2, 5, 7, 8, 12, 14, 20, 22, 27, 28, 33, 36, 42, 43, 44, 45, 48, 54, 58, 60, 66, 68, 69, 70, 75, 79, 86, 87, 90, 91, 92, 94, 95, 96, 98, 99

G

Generally Accepted Accounting Principles, 88
Glass-Steagall Act, 94
GLBA, 66
governance, 85
government securities, 27, 79
Government Sponsored Enterprises, 36
governments, vii, 22, 27, 35, 37, 43, 57, 96
Gramm-Leach-Bliley Act, 66, 71, 88, 89, 91, 93, 94, 99
growth, 9, 37, 72, 76
GSEs, 23, 26, 33, 36, 39, 50, 72, 76, 94, 101
guidance, 63
guidelines, 61

H

health, 37, 42, 52, 55, 58, 99
hedging, 94
height, 15
historical data, 62
history, 31, 45, 56
holding company, 40, 57, 63, 67, 70, 71, 89, 92, 93, 94, 99
homeowners, 26, 92
homes, 26, 37
host, 39, 50
House, 30, 33, 101
House of Representatives, 33
housing, 24, 39, 72
HUD, 63, 72

I

illiquid asset, 14
IMF, 11, 20, 30
imports, 79
income, 67, 96, 98
income tax, 67, 96
indirect effect, 8
individuals, 43, 91, 95, 96
industrialization, 12
industry(s), 26, 27, 28, 29, 30, 36, 39, 49, 52, 58, 63, 69, 71, 94, 98
inflation, 65, 91
information sharing, 74, 75
initiation, 93
inspectors, 52
institutions, viii, 4, 11, 13, 15, 18, 19, 20, 31, 32, 35, 41, 45, 49, 50, 51, 53, 56, 60, 65, 66, 67, 68, 70, 73, 75, 80, 81, 82, 87, 90, 91, 92, 93, 97, 99
interagency coordination, 75
interest rates, 13, 14, 17, 18, 19, 43, 44, 58, 59, 71, 86, 94
intermediaries, 3, 7, 8, 15, 16, 17, 19, 22, 23, 24, 29, 43, 68
internal controls, 58
International Monetary Fund, 11, 20

international standards, 61
investment(s), 7, 12, 18, 22, 30, 36, 42, 45, 48, 54, 56, 62, 67, 69, 70, 71, 72, 79, 82, 85, 87, 94, 95, 96, 99, 101
investment bank, 7, 42, 45, 67, 70, 71, 79, 94, 95, 99, 101
investors, vii, 2, 8, 12, 14, 16, 18, 22, 27, 28, 35, 42, 43, 46, 48, 60, 68, 69, 80, 94, 95, 96
isolation, 16
issues, 24, 25, 43, 48, 58, 61, 62, 65, 75, 79, 85, 86

J

job training, 37
jurisdiction, 38, 50, 66, 68, 70, 71, 75

L

laws, 43, 52, 55, 56, 57, 63, 64, 68, 69, 73, 79, 80, 89
lead, 22, 47, 62
legal protection, 26
legislation, 3, 28, 55, 60, 82
legislative proposals, 67
lender of last resort, 3, 4, 19, 21, 32, 36, 45, 67, 92
lending, 3, 7, 8, 15, 17, 19, 23, 24, 25, 36, 43, 44, 45, 47, 53, 56, 57, 59, 60, 62, 66, 70, 75, 82, 86, 95, 97, 98, 101
liquid assets, 16, 17, 95
liquidate, 96
liquidity, 3, 13, 14, 17, 19, 21, 22, 23, 24, 28, 30, 48, 53, 54, 58, 60, 70, 75, 79, 81, 87
literacy, 47
litigation, 58
loans, 2, 5, 7, 8, 9, 12, 13, 14, 15, 16, 17, 19, 22, 24, 25, 26, 31, 32, 37, 42, 43, 44, 45, 47, 48, 51, 56, 57, 59, 61, 63, 79, 82, 86, 90, 91, 92, 95, 96, 97, 98
low risk, 8

M

macroeconomic policy, 78
magnitude, vii, 1, 3, 25
man, 56, 96
management, 41, 57, 58, 60, 62, 63, 68, 72, 85, 86, 93
manipulation, 51, 71
manufacturing, 61
market failure, 38, 45
marketability, 85
marketing, 45, 94
marketplace, 92
matter, viii, 2, 35, 51
meat, 52
membership, 46, 51, 91, 97
metals, 56, 91, 94
mission(s), 39, 49, 71, 72
models, 62
modernization, 92
monetary policy, 30, 67
money supply, 36
monopoly, 100
moral hazard, 28, 33, 74, 96
mortgage-backed securities, 13, 16, 25, 79

N

New York Stock Exchange, 51, 98
nonbank lenders, vii, 1, 25

O

old age, 37
operations, 30, 70, 76, 79, 93, 95
organ, 101
organize, 42, 57
OSHA, 52
overlap, 49
oversight, 37, 50, 75, 85
ownership, 42, 72, 89, 90, 98

P

participants, 2, 4, 17, 26, 30, 32, 36, 38, 39, 45, 49, 51, 54, 62, 68, 69, 70, 71, 77, 78, 97, 100
PCA, 96
permit, 32, 77
pessimism, 62
playing, 68
policy, vii, 1, 2, 3, 4, 5, 7, 12, 14, 17, 18, 19, 20, 21, 23, 24, 29, 31, 37, 39, 40, 41, 43, 45, 46, 48, 49, 52, 55, 62, 75, 99
policy issues, 52, 62
policy options, 2, 23, 40
policy problems, 12, 31, 39, 41, 43, 46, 48, 49, 55
policy rate, 14
policy reform, 17
policy responses, vii, 4, 45, 46
policymakers, 3, 11, 20, 23, 46
pollution, 32
pools, 43, 48, 86, 94, 95, 96
portfolio, 22, 33, 58, 59, 60, 85
President, 38, 73, 75, 88, 101
primary function, 97
principles, 17, 20, 29, 63, 69, 75
private firms, 14, 80
probability, 62
professional qualifications, 46
professionals, 46
profit, 43, 67, 72, 89, 92, 96, 98
protection, 41, 55, 63, 72, 92, 94, 95, 97
prudential regulation, 29, 32, 39, 40, 48, 57, 79, 100
purchasing power, 47

R

race, 22
real estate, 18, 55, 63, 72, 73
reality, 56
recommendations, 30, 73, 74, 85, 89
Reform, 3, 17, 22, 32, 33, 36, 49, 65, 88, 101
regulations, vii, 1, 2, 3, 4, 18, 21, 28, 31, 32, 33, 40, 43, 45, 50, 51, 52, 58, 61, 63, 65, 75, 78, 82, 86, 89, 92
regulatory agencies, 38, 52
regulatory changes, 30, 74
regulatory framework, 26
regulatory oversight, 57
relative size, 11
repo, 7, 10, 11, 20, 21, 22, 48, 66
reputation, 32
requirements, 2, 3, 16, 18, 22, 28, 32, 36, 45, 57, 58, 59, 60, 61, 62, 67, 68, 69, 71, 77, 78, 80, 81, 82, 90, 91, 94, 100
resale, 79, 80, 95
researchers, 5, 29
reserves, 56, 60, 66, 82
resilience, 3, 16, 60
resolution, 26, 37, 53, 61, 63, 66, 74
resources, 42, 43, 44, 46, 93
response, 3, 12, 50, 57
responsiveness, 85
restaurants, 52
restoration, 76
restrictions, 12, 19, 31, 43, 45, 80
retail, 48, 79
retail deposit, 48
retirement, 37, 65
rewards, 47
risk management, 39, 58
risk profile, 84
risk-taking, 60, 70
rules, viii, 16, 23, 26, 27, 28, 32, 33, 35, 39, 43, 46, 49, 51, 52, 55, 58, 63, 68, 69, 71, 75, 77, 92, 97, 101

S

safe haven, 31
safe havens, 31
safety, 2, 18, 21, 22, 23, 26, 30, 32, 36, 40, 45, 52, 57, 58, 62, 63, 64, 65, 68, 70, 71, 72, 75, 81, 84, 92
savings, 12, 14, 19, 32, 47, 53, 64, 67, 87, 90, 91, 92, 97, 99
savings banks, 97

scope, 12, 43, 52, 85, 86
Secretary of the Treasury, 73, 75
Securities Exchange Act, 71
securities firms, 92, 94
securitisation, 30
segregation, 94
seller(s), 45, 46, 55, 73, 92, 93, 95
Senate, 49, 75
sensitivity, 75
service provider, 61
services, 4, 7, 8, 12, 20, 32, 42, 43, 45, 46, 50, 53, 56, 62, 63, 67, 72, 73, 89, 92, 94, 95, 97, 98
severe stress, 21
shadow banking, vii, 1, 2, 3, 4, 5, 6, 7, 9, 10, 11, 12, 14, 15, 16, 17, 18, 19, 20, 29, 30, 31, 32, 47, 48, 60, 98
short-term interest rate, 43
signs, 48
single market, 41
skin, 47
small firms, 80
social costs, 32
society, 37
solution, 37
speculation, 71
speech, 30, 31
spot market, 46
stability, 4, 51, 66, 74, 86
stabilization, 28
stars, 6
state(s), 12, 31, 50, 52, 53, 57, 64, 66, 67, 74, 86, 89, 90, 91, 92, 93, 95, 96, 98
statistics, 32
statutes, 63, 82, 89
statutory authority, 69, 70
stock, 52, 69, 71, 72, 75, 80, 86, 91
stock exchange, 69
stock price, 52, 86
stockholders, 40, 56, 81, 82
stress, 28, 62
stress test, 62
structure, 11, 37, 42, 57, 63, 70, 82, 90, 93, 100
substitutes, 3, 6, 29, 31
supervision, 32, 61, 69, 71, 76, 99, 101
supervisor(s), 57, 72, 74, 100
surplus, 26
surveillance, 64
susceptibility, 76
sustainability, 85
systemic risk, 16, 22, 23, 37, 39, 40, 51, 53, 64, 65, 70, 72, 74, 76, 99, 100

T

tactics, 59
target, 78
Task Force, 75
taxes, 32, 96
taxpayers, 60
techniques, 22, 61
technologies, 92
telephone, 96
tension, 60
threats, 51, 74
thrifts, 9, 14, 39, 54, 57, 64, 65, 66, 82, 97
time deposits, 82
time periods, 21
Title I, 2, 21, 22, 23, 26, 71, 73, 80
Title II, 2, 22, 23
Title V, 26, 73, 81
trade, 4, 50, 78, 91, 92, 95
trade-off, 4, 50
training, 58
tranches, 25, 96
transactions, viii, 15, 20, 21, 22, 23, 30, 35, 39, 40, 58, 62, 78, 79, 89, 90, 96
transformation, 3, 32, 43
Treasury, 9, 23, 26, 27, 31, 36, 45, 53, 72, 76, 79
Treasury Secretary, 53
treatment, 25, 67, 96
turnover, 78

U

U.S. Department of the Treasury, 93, 100

U.S. Treasury, 9, 14, 20, 45, 48, 69, 72, 77, 79, 95
underwriting, 64, 94
unions, 9, 39, 54, 57, 65, 67, 82, 87, 91
United, 9, 10, 11, 12, 19, 31, 37, 38, 40, 42, 45, 49, 50, 55, 66, 67, 78, 93, 95, 96, 99
United Kingdom (UK), 50
United States, 9, 10, 11, 12, 19, 31, 37, 38, 40, 42, 45, 49, 55, 66, 67, 78, 93, 95, 96, 99

V

variables, 71
variations, 56
vehicles, 12, 24, 30
venture capital, 80
venue, 45, 47
volatility, 43, 52
Volcker Rule, 79, 99
vote, 74
voting, 64, 73
vulnerability, 13, 21

W

Washington, 33
wealth, 62
websites, 55, 89
White Paper, 32
withdrawal, 28, 44, 65
worldwide, 61
wrongdoing, 58
WTO, 61